D1598040

HOSPITALITY
& RESTAURANT DESIGN
No.2

Roger Yee

Visual Reference Publications Inc., New York

Copyright © 2001 by Visual Reference Publications, Inc.

All rights reserved. No part of this book may be reproduced in any form or by any electronic or mechanical means, including information storage and retrieval systems, without permission in writing from the publisher.

Visual Reference Publications, Inc.
302 Fifth Avenue
New York, NY 10001

Distributors to the trade in the United States and Canada
Watson-Guptill
770 Broadway
New York, NY 10003

Distributors outside the United States and Canada
HarperCollins International
10 East 53 Street
New York, NY 10022-5299

Book Design: Harish Patel Design Associates, New York

Library of Congress Cataloging in Publication Data:
Hospitality & Restaurant Design No.2
Printed in Hong Kong
ISBN 1-58471-019-5

Contents

Introduction

Photographs of travelers taken a century ago depict a nomadic life that looks familiar and exotic to us now. Wealthy guests of grand hotels brought entourages that included armies of servants and baggage galore, because they insisted on having goods and services that might not be found at their destinations. When they went to dinner at opulent, full-service restaurants, they ordered multiple courses of fine food and drink just as their modern counterparts do, but they consumed quantities that would shock our diet-conscious society.

One hundred years later, the rich don't need the caravans. Professionally trained travel industry personnel minister to their needs wherever charge cards are accepted. As for packing everything but the kitchen sink, global transportation networks can ship products any place at any time. High-end hotels and restaurants remain as grand as ever. However, the food portions are much smaller.

The poor could never count on room and board when traveling. What they found—if they found anything—was grim at best. The establishments that served them circa 1900 have their counterparts in 2000.

Yet hotels and restaurants at every price point improved during the 20th century, and the transformation could be seen in their design. Since the industrial age brought unprecedented prosperity to much of the developed world, pleasure became as basic a reason for travel as work. This prompted hoteliers and restaurateurs to develop new facilities for middle class guests to give them comfort and entertainment as well as convenience, raising the quality of design and technology.

Admittedly, the current wave of consolidation among hotels and restaurants is a mixed blessing for design. The disappearance of mom-and-pop businesses is obliterating much of the diversity and authenticity of enterprises that flourished despite (or by virtue of) their local idiosyncrasies. Who will venture to build new hotels shaped like wigwams now, or serve culinary mysteries on mismatched china?

Design created for mass-marketed hotel and restaurant franchises is not inherently bad design. Many travelers want a familiar, comfortable and affordable place to stay or dine, and international chains deliver this kind of product extremely well. Not only have they developed standards for architecture and interior design that range from acceptable to exceptional, they enjoy economies of scale and efficiencies of operation to dress their spaces better than many a mom-and-pop ever did.

Over the long term, hotel and restaurant design will gain from the public's growing sophistication. Customers at all price points will expect more benefits as competition heightens, and hoteliers and restaurateurs will find ways to give them more, targeting good design as one of the most visible benefits. Small enterprises and start-ups will probably lead in design innovation, since distinctive design can instantly place them on the map. But the giants will not be far behind. Today's traveler needn't be rich to exercise the power of choice, as is shown by the talented architects and interior designers whose work appears on the following pages.

Roger Yee
Editor

Foreword

There was a time when hospitality designers worked in almost perfect anonymity. When hotels were either ornately grand or simply functional, and restaurants as predictable as the food they were serving—the bland leading the bland—few took notice of the names behind the projects, since so many of them looked alike.

But oh, what a difference a passage of time can make. As a more sophisticated and well-traveled public started demanding more from the places they stayed and dined, the importance of environment became paramount. Gradually, designers began to move to the forefront, too, just as great chefs did, taking their places as equally important as anyone else to the total hospitality experience. Enter any prominent restaurant or hotel today and ask who designed the space; chances are, you'll be told. Some restaurants are even marking the designer's name on the menu, as prominently displayed as the superstar chef.

Walking through the pages that follow reveals myriad reasons why such celebrity is apropos. Project after project explodes from the page with creativity, color, adventure, even wit. The unique challenges of hospitality design are met time and again with a seemingly inexhaustible wellspring of inventiveness.

Whether you're a client seeking a visual resume, a designer looking for inspiration, or simply a civilian drawn to the beauty of interior design, this book is certain to hit its mark. Know that the designers represented—happily, anonymous no more—are working at full tilt to create what may be the industry's Golden Age.

Michael Adams
Hospitality Design Magazine

Alexandra Champalimaud & Associates Inc.

1 Union Square West
Suite 603
New York, New York 10003
212.807.8869
212.807.1742 (Fax)

Alexandra Champalimaud & Associates Inc.

ParkGate
Dallas, Texas

Left: *The main lobby lounge at ParkGate rivals luxury hotels.*
Below left: *A typical residence for active senior living.*
Below right: *The library is for reading and quiet conversation.*
Photography: *J. Benoist Photographic*

Growing old gracefully is giving way in the 21st century to growing old vigorously. As a consequence, housing for seniors leading active lifestyles now provides an alternative to the more sedate and institutional-style senior residence that has been the norm. A good example is ParkGate in Dallas, which Alexandra Champalimaud & Associates recently converted from a mid-century, multi-story, landmark Modernist corporate facility into an exclusive residence for independent, active seniors seeking the convenience of a centralized community. Embracing the existing Modernist structure as a vision for retirement living, the designers placed 46 dwelling units, ranging from studios to one- and two-bedroom residences, on the upper floors for privacy, while public spaces were located downstairs to observe the bustle of the city. The design accentuated the contrasts, so the ground floor's lofty elevations were dramatized through rich colors, bold graphic patterns and furniture grouped in intimate clusters, while a gracious and understated mood was evoked upstairs by sumptuous materials-like polished wood, stone, custom tile and carpeting—in finely detailed combinations. Senior living at ParkGate is certainly not our great-grandparents' idea of retirement. It's livelier-and probably a lot more fun.

Above: Dining at ParkGate offers a restaurant ambiance.
Near right: Residents may prepare meals in their own kitchenettes.
Far right: A welcoming conversation pit with fireplace.

Alexandra Champalimaud & Associates Inc.

The Algonquin Hotel
New York, New York

Left: Edwardian-style entrance and canopy, steps from Times Square. **Below left:** Fabled main lobby and lounge, a beacon for literati. **Bottom:** Front desk, showing new mural above wainscoting. **Photography:** Scott Frances

In New York City's literary world, the phrase "Only at the New Yorker" was synonymous in the 20th century with "Only at the Algonquin." A fondness for the favored watering place of Robert Benchley, Dorothy Parker, James Thurber and other writers of the New Yorker magazine's legendary Round Table persists to this day. Now it is faithfully acknowledged in a renovation of the 12-story, 165-room establishment by Alexandra Champalimaud & Associates for British hotelier Ian Lloyd-Jones, a 1998 Gold Key Finalist. To retain the brilliant, cosmopolitan spirit, the designers reconciled guests' needs for modern services with the design ethos of the legendary years from the opening in 1902, at the close of the Edwardian era, to the Round Table talks (around a 7-foot diameter oak table) in the 1920's, at the height of the Jazz Age. Archival photography and press clippings helped document the changing scene, so new interiors could combine restored details, such as ebony-stained wainscoting, upholstered furniture and plaster ceilings, with new furniture (including antiques), carpet and lighting, all served by the latest in building technology and guest services. A century later, it's still "Only at the Algonquin."

12

Below: Bath accommo-
dations offer period
appointments.
Bottom: A seating area
in main lobby is framed
in fine woodwork.

bove: Guest rooms
recall the Algonquin's
fabled early decades.

13

Alexandra Champalimaud & Associates Inc.

Le Chateau Frontenac
Quebec City, Quebec, Canada

Right: Sweeping windows provide a panoramic view.
Below: A richly detailed lounge with Jacobean furnishings.
Photography: Claude-Simon Langlois.

Right: A typical gue-
stroom.
Below: The front desk
in full architectural
dress.
Bottom: Window detail
at main lobby lounge.

Winner of the 1999 Gold
Key Grand Prize, Le
Chateau Frontenac is a
beloved landmark that
has been restored and
refurbished as befits a
proud symbol of Quebec
City. Alexandra
Champalimaud &
Associates was commis-
sioned by Canadian
Pacific Hotels & Resorts
to revive the 605-room
Chateau, built in the
style of a grand castle in

the Loire Valley from an original design by W.S. Maxwell at the turn of the century, with an interior design that recalls the hotel's classic style in the 1920s and 1930s. The physical environment had to accommodate contemporary operations for tour groups of all sizes, yet sustain the Old World aura that has endeared the hotel to generations of guests. Drawing on the historic architecture for inspiration, the designers developed a scheme to preserve and revive what was in sound condition, such as the richly stenciled ceiling beams, architectural wood paneling and period lighting fixtures, and to bring guest facilities into the 21st century with new furniture, fabrics, custom-designed carpets and other appropriate furnishings. Of course, the latest in building technology and guest services would be discreetly present too. Why shouldn't guests be able to surround themselves in the timeless charm of Le Chateau Frontenac, confident that they are sampling the best of Quebec City's past and present?

Above right: *The pool offers modern comforts with Old World charm.*
Below right: *A restaurant that recalls the great Loire Valley castles.*

Aria Group Architects, Inc.

1100 West Lake Street
Suite 140
Oak Park, Illinois 60301
708.445.8400
708.445.1788 (Fax)
www.ariainc.com

Aria Group Architects, Inc.

Blue Chip Casino & Hotel
Michigan City, Indiana

Above right: *Blue Chip's Modernist exterior elevations.*
Right: *Art Deco-style main atrium in docking pavilion.*
Photography: *Steve Hall, Hedrich Blessing; Doug Snower, Doug Snower Photography*

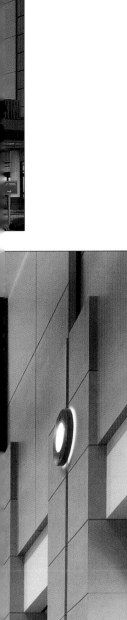

Right: Detail of 50-foot high main atrium.

Michigan City has drawn vacationers to its sandy dunes and beaches for years, and some recent additions, including the Lighthouse Mall and now the Blue Chip Casino & Hotel, are helping to revive this charming community. Since the site of the Blue Chip, a stretch of abandoned homes along Trail Creek, had no architectural context to influence the design by Aria Group Architects, Inc., the buildings received clean Modernist exteriors and rich Art Deco-style interiors. Custom-designed and standard furnishings were combined to create a uniquely exciting Art Deco environment that recalls the frivolity of the Roaring Twenties in connecting three components, a floating casino, mandated by law and not designed by Aria Group, a docking pavilion and a 200-room hotel, another legal requirement, into one very compelling reason to visit Michigan City today.

Above: A view of hotel lobby, which is airy, spacious yet inviting.
Below: Bar detail, part of a 280-seat buffet, 80-seat bistro and 150-seat lounge.

Aria Group Architects, Inc.

Brookfield Zoo
Brookfield, Illinois

Zoos are learning to compete for consumers' leisure time and money by introducing and upgrading such crowd-pleasing amenities as food services, gift shops and live events. The new Brookfield Zoo Living Coast Guest Services Building in Brookfield, Illinois, designed by Aria Group Architects, Inc., does this in a graceful, 21,000-square foot curvilinear structure that welcomes visitors to its outdoor European-style piazza, where people gather for entertainment and events, and its soaring indoor atrium servery. Not only is there room for 100 in an informal dining room and 180 in an upstairs full-service tapas restaurant that can be converted into space for one to three classrooms, the people-friendly facility also has a gift shop, restrooms and an outdoor garden dining area for 250. Stylistically, the architecture marks a transition between NeoClassical structures in the old zoo and International Style facilities at the new Living Coast exhibit, but visitors can appreciate its charms regardless of aesthetic labels.

Top: Exterior of Living Coast Guest Services.
Above: Atrium servery.
Right: The gift shop.
Photography: Doug Snower, Doug Snower Photography

Below: *The 180-seat, full-service tapas "cantina" restaurant on the second floor.*

Aria Group Architects, Inc.

Lettuce Entertain You Enterprises
Chicago and Boston

Right: *Wildfire, Oak Brook, Illinois.*
Below: *Corner Bakery, Chicago.*
Below right: *Big Bowl, Lincolnshire, Illinois.*
Bottom right: *Brasserie Jo, Boston.*
Opposite page: *Ben Pao, Chicago.*
Photography: *Warren Jagger (Brasserie Jo); Mark Ballogg, Steinkamp/Ballogg*

Keeping pace with gifted Chicago restaurateur Rich Melman and his Lettuce Entertain You Enterprises Inc. to develop over 50 restaurants, including 24 new concepts, has challenged Aria Group Architects, Inc. to bring fresh thinking and new ideas to the hospitality industry since 1989. Maintaining the appeal of existing restaurants and creating new concepts that stand out from the crowd is a daily requirement for Lettuce Entertain You Enterprises in 13 states, Europe and Asia, since customers in all these markets face new choices all the time. Aria Group Architects is proud of the exceptional dining environments it has designed for Lettuce Entertain You Enterprises.

Aria Group Architects, Inc.

Brio Cocina Espana
Chicago, Illinois

Can Spain be just minutes away in Chicago's River North? The neighborhood has become known for creative businesses and adventurous dining and entertainment, so a full-service, 200-seat restaurant like Brio Cocina Espana was almost destined to arrive, serving Spanish cuisine. Intriguing as the food is, the design by Aria Group Architects, Inc. also salutes the organic architecture of the Iberian peninsula, which shows marvelous vigor today. Yet the restaurant's sensual forms came only after a thorough reworking of the existing, choppy space into functional zones, blending such diverse elements as Spanish tiles, a hand-crafted zinc bar top, existing heavy timber structure, oversized vinyl floor tiles and contem-porary, organic-shaped furnishings into a tantalizing vision of contemporary Spain that just happens to be north of the Chicago River.

Above: *The zinc bar at the front of the house.*
Above right: *Heavy timber contrasts with graceful soffits and furnishings.*
Right: *Banquettes define the dining room.*
Photography: *Doug Snower, Doug Snower Photography*

Arnold Syrop Associates, Architects

290 Fifth Avenue

New York

New York 10001

212.947.7070

212.643.8449 (Fax)

asyrop@earthlink.net

Arnold Syrop Associates, Architects

Maloney & Porcelli
New York, New York

Left: *The main dining room and mezzanine flow dynamically together.* **Below left:** *Placing the bar in the center enlivens the entire restaurant.* **Opposite:** *Coat closets along the mezzanine staircase produce entertaining activity.* **Photography:** *Peter Paige,*

Guests may never see a plaque proclaiming "steakhouse for the millennium" as they enter Maloney & Porcelli, a bustling new Manhattan restaurant designed by Arnold Syrop Associates, Architects. Yet the phrase might draw a smile from restaurateur Alan Stillman, whose highly successful Smith & Wolensky Restaurant Group already includes traditional steakhouses among the restaurants it owns and operates. Standard versions of this enduring genre honor men's clubs of the late 19th and early 20th centuries. Maloney & Porcelli, by contrast, is younger and livelier in spirit. A bolder, more contemporary sense of space is expressed in the clubby, 206-seat, three-story facility, highlighted by a main floor with a racetrack-style bar in the center, a mezzanine with two chef's table rooms boasting front-row kitchen views, and a lofty, third-level function space, the Skylight Room. But the steakhouse is also enjoyable in ways that all good restaurants are. There is handsome comfort in the beige, green and dark wood interior. There are fresh interpretations of historic American furnishings complemented by a fine collection of American folk art and illuminated by informal and intimate lighting fixtures. There is effortless entertainment in everyday activity, including the lively congeniality at the 20-seat bar, the flurry of waiters dashing to coat closets lining the mezzanine staircase to retrieve guests' belongings, and the hustle and bustle of the kitchen. And there is a popular menu with timely surprises—like crackling pork shank—that proves this restaurant is no flash in the pan.

Arnold Syrop Associates, Architects

The Restaurants at The Portofino Bay Hotel at UNIVERSAL Orlando℠, a Loews Hotel

Right: Welcome to family-style dining at the dining rooms of Mama Della's Ristorante℠.
Above left: A breakfront and unmatched chairs add to Mama Della's homey ambiance.
Above right: Classical columns help define the palazzo-style formality of Delfino Riviera℠.
Photography: Courtesy UNIVERSAL Orlando.

Gourmets know that domestic versions of foreign cuisine veer from the real thing when restaurateurs hesitate to take customers into unfamiliar culinary territory. The same concern haunts theme park operators and hoteliers. A satisfying compromise can be enjoyed by customers of the seven restaurants and bars and a bakery designed by Arnold Syrop Associates, Architects, for The Portofino Bay Hotel at UNIVERSAL Orlando℠, a Loews Hotel. Knowing that many visitors would not be familiar with Portofino, the famed coastal resort town on Italy's Ligurian Sea, the designers blended authentic themes with the public's expectations to make each dining experience feel like a standalone enterprise—and nothing like a typical "hotel restaurant." The informal, 270-seat Trattoria del Porto℠, for example, persuades guests that it represents a converted warehouse that was renovated "decades ago." Entering 140-seat Mama Della's Ristorante℠, by contrast, is like being invited to an Italian home, complete with wood-beam ceilings, ceramic tile and wood plank floors, a variety of wallcoverings and chairs that don't match. As for 140-seat Delfino Riviera℠, the dream of feasting in a fabled, 17th-century palazzo with a harbor view becomes a daily reality here.

Above: Trattoria del Porto℠ imagines itself a warehouse conversion from "decades ago."
Right: A closeup of a column shows the attention to detail needed for a convincing atmosphere.

Arnold Syrop Associates, Architects

Roy's New York
New York, New York

Right: The semi-circular exhibition kitchen offers a vivacious focus for the entire restaurant.
Below: A second area of activity that sustains the lively feeling at Roy's is its semi-circular bar.
Below right: Like the exhibition kitchen, the bar is enhanced by its own soffit and reveal.
Opposite: Novel in New York's financial district is Roy's light, airy and festive dining room.
Photography: Paul Warchol

Roy Yamaguchi, a Japanese-born Hawaiian chef, has become a celebrity by inventing distinctive dishes blending Asian and Western cooking. Now New York's financial district can sample his mahi-mahi with a macadamian nut crust and Kona lobster basil sauce at 226-seat Roy's New York, designed by Arnold Syrop Associates, Architects, and located in Marriott Financial Center Hotel. The 6,000-square foot addition to the Roy's chain represents a first for Marriott, which had not partnered with an independent restaurateur or design firm before. In addition, the design breaks with Wall Street's formal, dark and masculine eateries by introducing a destination that is light, airy and festive for sophisticated customers coming from Wall Street and the city at large. Its expansive dining room focuses on two islands of activity, Roy's trademark exhibition kitchen and a bar, each semi-circular in shape, ringed with seats and highlighted by matching soffit and cove-lighted reveal, as

Below: A sensitive lighting scheme keeps the lighting in step with the moods of breakfast, lunch and dinner at Roy's.

Right: Custom fixtures accent the restaurant by acknowledging Asian sources without mimicking them.

well as a double row of columns ornamented with colorful murals that seems to radiate their own light. Materials and furnishings that include blond wood floors, cherrywood furniture and millwork, and custom lighting fixtures draw inspiration from Asian art without copying it. Everything glows under a lighting scheme that changes from the bright cheerful room for hotel breakfasts to the chic night spot for romatic dinners. Crowds waiting in line for dinners and Saturdays are an eloquent rejoinder to Rudyard Kipling that between East and West the twain has met—at Roy's.

Backen & Gillam Architects

2352 Marinship Way
Sausalito, California 94965
415.289.3860
415.289.3866 (Fax)

1028 Main Street
St. Helena, California 94574
707.967.1920
707.967.1924 (Fax)

Backen & Gillam Architects

Edgewood Winery
St. Helena, California

Contradictory as the practice may be, northern California's Napa Valley pays homage to centuries of wine making with buildings that all too often proclaim how new they are. Edgewood Winery was determined to avoid this fate in retaining Backen & Gillam Architects for the exterior renovation and interior design of its 2,860-square foot Office and Wine-Tasting Room in St. Helena. The facility was already set back from the road along a path lined with small agricultural buildings that enhanced its rustic charm. Edgewood Winery wanted the remodeling to visually reinforce its ties to the land and its commitment to the wine making tradition. To give the exterior an historic, vernacular image, the architects resurfaced the facades with a stone base of petrified seashore and Monterey sandstone, redwood plank siding that was put through an aging

Top: Exterior of Office and Wine Tasting Room.
Above: Landscape at Edgewood Winery.
Left: Looking inside past sliding barn doors.
Photography: David Duncan Livingston

process to obtain a weathered look, limestone quoins, and redwood recycled from wine casks that was used to fabricate the large, sliding redwood barn doors, shutters, vents and cupolas. The same imagery was carried indoors with more recycled redwood, which the architects applied to the casework, ceiling planking and wine bar, tinted concrete floors inset among antique wood planking borders, antique rugs, a seating area of casual wicker grouped around a wood-burning stove, shaded lamps, and iron hardware. Naturally the focus of the facility was on the wine bar, a simple yet elegant form fabricated from a solid piece of timber 12 inches x 14 inches x 26 feet set on an iron frame and backed by a finely detailed redwood wall of wine bottles. Visitors coming to taste the glories of Napa Valley will surely pause here to toast Edgewood Winery.

Backen & Gillam Architects

Kokkari Restaurant
San Francisco, California

Only minutes from the Financial District, San Franciscans have discovered what looks like a timeless but hitherto unknown Greek restaurant called Kokkari, designed by Backen & Gillam Architects. All the details speak of enduring Old World virtues: rustic wood and upholstered furniture, antique wall tapestries, antique rugs over plank flooring, rough-hewn wood beamed ceilings, warm, plaster walls, and rawhide shaded table lamps and floor lamps. It's becoming a favored place to sample Greek ethnic dishes, which are not widely available in the City by the Bay. Yet, like many memorable restaurants before it, Kokkari originated not long ago as a raw space that was vacated by another restaurant. The designers restructured what had been a problematic shell by completely gutting the basement to support a kitchen, private dining room and bathrooms, and introducing a tempting sequence of spaces to draw customers inside. Who can resist proceeding from a cozy Front Bar/Lounge with a roaring fireplace and rotisserie past a

monumental Greek urn for slow brewing traditional coffee to the Main Dining Room, where you may sit at a 16-seat family-style dining table before a gleaming Exhibition Kitchen to watch Greek cooking?

Top: *A view of the Front Bar/Lounge.*
Above: *Family-style dining table and standard settings.*
Opposite: *Main Dining Room with Greek urn.*
Photography: *David Duncan Livingston*

36

Backen & Gillam Architects

Stars Restaurant
San Francisco, California

Below: *Walnut case-work shapes seating arrangements.*
Photography: *David Duncan Livingston, Mark C. Darley (below right only)*

How do you update a culinary legend? When the subject was Stars, a beloved San Francisco restaurant founded by legendary restaurateur Jeremiah Tower in the mid-1980's, managing partner Stanley Morris asked Backen & Gillam Architects to incorporate the best of what existed in an intriguing new environment. The catch: Construction would be finished in two weeks on a modest budget. Thus, the 270-seat, 4,800-square foot Stars was reinvented through a series of bold, decisive and economical changes. Among the highlights of the new scheme were a new seating arrangement to provide a more intimate experience, new casework in dark walnut with stainless steel accents, concentrated in the center of the dining room to comple- ment existing mahogany wainscoting and a hand- some bar, new, ebonized wood flooring with Persian-style area rugs, and new, massive murals by San Francisco artist Charley Brown depicting fresh produce. The new owners and the archi- tects were well aware how closely their work would be scrutinized by patrons coming from the nearby opera and sym- phony. As a conse-

Below: *A massive mural by artist Charley Brown sets an irrepressible mood.*

39

quence, every visible detail was studied, including the plush velour on chairs and leather in booths, rich yellow walls and paneled ceilings, rawhide lamp shades and custom iron chandeliers, sheer draperies and newly open kitchen displaying a new pizza oven and rotisserie. Add to this a new chef and menu, and you have what San Franciscans declare to be the Stars they have always loved—and continue to love.

Right: *Another Charley Brown mural anchors an intimate gathering.*
Below: *A different city, a different look, for Stars in Seattle.*

Bogdanow
Partners Architects, PC

75 Spring Street
New York
New York 10012
212.966.0313
212.941.8875 (Fax)
www.bogdanow.com

Bogdanow Partners Architects, PC

Merchants NY
New York, New York

Left: *Bar and main dining room.*
Above: *Downstairs cigar bar.*
Photography: *Peter Aaron/Esto*

Hard-working yet hedonistic, team-spirited yet focused on friends, independent yet eager to network, Gen Xers are the targets of Merchants NY, designed by Bogdanow Partners Architects to be their oasis on Manhattan's Upper East Side. In fact, single professionals, age 27 years and above, regularly fill the 190-seat, 7,000-square foot bar, restaurant and cigar lounge in search of the in crowd, the big deal or simply The One. Making this happen took effort. First, the facility's two floors were visibly connected when a small, street-level landing was expanded for a winding staircase leading to a bar, main dining room, smaller living room and private dining nook upstairs, and a cigar bar and smaller lounges downstairs. Then an emphatically linear interior design, whose superb detailing—including wrought iron grillwork, glass and wood doors, coffered ceilings, domes with gold and fiber optic stars, intricately patterned floors of terrazzo and carpet, elegant vitrines and richly upholstered furniture—recalls the Vienna Sesession, Arts and Crafts movement and 1930s oceanliners, gave the space the sumptuous character Gen Xers have claimed as their own.

Right: Downstairs lounge.
Below: Living room on the upper floor.

Bogdanow Partners
Architects, PC

Legal Sea Foods
Boston, Massachusetts

Proper Bostonians know their sea food, and Legal Sea Foods restaurants are among their favorite settings for scrod, mahi mahi or the catch of the day. What makes the latest flagship, the 400-seat, 14,000-square foot Park Square Motor Mart Legal Sea Foods, designed by Bogdanow Partners Architects, stand out is its bold, appealing departure from the chain's beloved, 19th-century look. The new design, inside a restored Art Deco parking garage, exchanges man's view of the sea for nature's look at herself. Customers enter a series of strikingly beautiful dining rooms at street level that combine sleek wall planes of anigre wood, floors of safari quartzite and Douglas fir, a copper mesh ceiling tracing an undulating soffit, banquette seating in richly patterned fabrics, and columns sheathed in art glass with the photo murals of acclaimed deep-sea photographer David Doubilet. If they descend a steel-and-blue-stone staircase adjacent to an iridescent oyster bar and large fish tank, they may take their places at a stunning bar/lounge featuring additional banquette seating and events rooms. The preliminary verdict: Proper Bostonians love it all.

Left: *Steel-and-blue-stone staircase.*
Right: *View towards oyster bar.*
Above: *Photo mural-framed doorway.*
Opposite: *Main dining floor.*
Photography: *Warren Jagger*

Bogdanow Partners
Architects, PC

Tribeca Grand Hotel
New York, New York

You don't have to convince the art-and-fashion-forward New York neighborhoods of Soho and Tribeca that design sells, so when the owners of the Soho Grand Hotel developed a second hotel four blocks away in Tribeca, they asked Bogdanow Partners Architects for a strong, dramatic lobby design to complement the in-house architecture. The result is a triangular structure with a central atrium whose 10,000-square foot first floor serves as reception, lounge, waiting room, restaurant, bar and meeting place. Inspiration for the Tribeca Grand Hotel came from the Industrial Age, Tribeca and Denver's Brown Palace Hotel, and is visible in the exposed trusses, glass cage elevators, custom ironwork, and curving, stainless steel screen that is lit with a wave light projector. The vibrant interior areas, enriched by such custom-designed features as the tailored lobby furniture, expansive tile-and-wood hearth, and soaring glass canopy over the bar, are subtly defined by furniture groupings, changes in floor surfaces and varied lighting designs. A reminder of the exclusivity that sustains this neighborhood is the 94-seat private screening room downstairs. But you already knew about that, didn't you?

Above: Private screening room.
Right: Hotel lobby restaurant.
Photography: Michael Kleinberg

Above left: Hotel lobby
from the bar.
Above: Central atrium
skylight.
Right: Tile-and-wood
hearth.

47

Bogdanow Partners
Architects, PC

American Park at the Battery
New York, New York

Above: *Exterior at night.*
Right: *Main dining room.*
Photography: *Dub Rogers*

This building, built in the Modernist Style in 1951, was originally the ticket sales rotunda for the Statue of Liberty before it was a Parks Department maintenance shed. The tower on the right is still a working vent for the Brooklyn Battery Tunnel. Now the 350-seat, 9,000-square foot American Park restaurant, designed by Bogdanow Partners Architects, offers its dramatic views of New York Harbor and the Statue to dinners. Working with numerous public and private agencies, the design firm has expanded the original 4,500-square foot structure by adding a second floor of dining/catering space and terraces. On the ground floor, generous windows and French doors frame an inventive series of seating and serving arrangements, including a main dining room of banquettes, booths and freestanding tables, a bar, a food bar, an open kitchen, and an indoor reflecting pool that greets guests at the entry, all appointed in natural materials, with a 100-seat patio outdoors. The two floors are joined by a grand spiral staircase—a crowning touch for a former ticket sales rotunda and maintenance building.

Brennan Beer Gorman
Monk / Interiors

515 Madison Avenue

New York

New York 10022

212.888.7667

212.935.3868 (Fax)

www.bbg-bbgm.com

1030 15th Street NW

Suite 900

Washington, DC 20005

202.452.1644

202.452.1647 (Fax)

Brennan Beer Gorman Monk / Architects & Interiors

Caribe Hilton
San Juan, Puerto Rico

Not since opening in 1949 had the respected, 17-acre Caribe Hilton in San Juan closed for extensive renovations—until the start of a recent, $60-million, nine-month project with Brennan Beer Gorman Monk. Although the island's first International Style hotel, designed by Osvaldo Torro and Miguel Ferrer, had seen many additions, the accumulated warren of breezeways and facilities no longer reflected the spirit of the original, streamlined interiors and ocean views. Restoring the openness was a major objective, along with new guest and group entrances, reconfigured lobby, newly designed and relocated public areas, additions to over 65,000 square feet of meeting space, including a new ballroom, remodeled restaurants and lounges, and 644 redesigned guestrooms. The return to the International Style has produced such dramatic rewards as the clear glass wall opposite the main entry in the lobby, showing arriving guests a sweeping view of the ocean. It has also created invigorating interiors highlighted by geometric-patterned textiles and carpets, elegantly simple furniture, custom lighting fixtures, and guestrooms with two-line telephone service, voice mail and data ports. The Caribe Hilton is over 50 years old—if you can believe it.

Above: Main Lobby looks out on the sea.
Above right: Pool Bar is a small architectural gem.
Right: Guestroom blends island charm with modern convenience.
Photography: Ron Blunt

Above: *Moonlight Bar casts spell that brings guests back.*
Right: *Meeting Room brings business to the beach.*

Brennan Beer Gorman Monk / Interiors

The Inn at Penn
Philadelphia, Pennsylvania

Left: Faculty Club is sunny and inviting.
Lower left: Living Room draws guests for socializing and conversation.
Bottom left: The Ivy Grille offers a fresh take on tradition.
Photography: Tom Crane

A great university attracts accomplished people much as honey attracts bees, and the University of Pennsylvania knew this in developing the newly opened Inn at Penn on its Philadelphia campus with Brennan Beer Gorman Monk. The Inn represents the hospitality component of the University's new mixed-use complex, Sansom Common, which contains 238 guestrooms, lobby registration, a 40-seat lobby lounge, a 120-seat street-level café, The Ivy Grille, the 250-seat Faculty Club, and a conference center with a ballroom, eight meeting rooms, two large pre-function areas and a 16-seat boardroom. What distinguishes the Inn is its need to serve both the University and the public. Though faculty, visiting professors and families of students would be regular patrons, the University knew that local residents, patrons of the arts and tourists could be expected as well. The interior respects the University's Arts & Crafts tradition by skillfully combining such materials as American white oak, traditional furnishings, distressed leather, Moravian tile, patterned tin ceilings and wrought-iron detailing to make the Inn, located at Walnut Street between 36th and 37th Streets, seem like the time-honored gathering place it will someday be.

52

Right: Lobby is a vital crossroads for faculty and guests.
Below: Guestroom provides gracious, timeless comfort.

Brennan Beer Gorman Monk / Interiors

Hotel Sofitel Philadelphia
Philadelphia, Pennsylvania

Left: *Chez Colette honors the famed author of Gigi.*
Above: *Lobby's barrel vaulted ceiling is reflected in the guilt-patterned floor.*
Photography: *Tom Crane*

Right: Ballroom anchors extensive meeting facilities.
Bottom: Meeting Room comes with full technical capabilities.

Is there life for a 188,000-square foot Philadelphia office building after the office workers depart? For the new, 306-room, 14-story Hotel Sofitel Philadelphia, designed by Brennan Beer Gorman/Architects and Brennan Beer Gorman Monk/Interiors, the answer is: Mais oui! The hotel combines the former Philadelphia Stock Exchange Building of 1964 with a 90,000-square foot addition. On the exterior, the existing limestone, pre-cast concrete and glass façade has been refurbished to contrast with the addition's glass curtain wall. Inside, guests now enter a splendid hotel inspired by 19th-century Shaker design. Anchored by a grand staircase joining three levels of public space (including a 5,000-square foot ballroom, nine meeting rooms, two private dining rooms, a video conference facility and pre-function area), the lobby features wood-sheathed columns, gleaming stone floor and dramatic, barrel-vaulted ceiling, and a richly upholstered lobby lounge. Other reasons the hotel won't be mistaken for an office building include Chez Colette, a vibrant, 100-seat brasserie and Sofitel trademark

named for the celebrated writer and furnished with banquette seating, clear glass dividers and cherry wood walls, and guestrooms featuring custom-designed casegoods, fine fabrics and carpets, warm indirect lighting, original artwork, baths with oversized tubs and glass-enclosed showers, and desk lamps on partners desks offering every telecommunications outlet for the Internet age. Now that's a hotel.

Top: *Junior Suite showcases fine furnishings in an elegant setting.*
Left: *Guest bathroom has residential ambiance.*
Above: *Guestroom boasts every amenity plus Internet link.*

Connie Beale, Inc.

6 Glenville Street

Greenwich, Connecticut 06831

203.532.4760

203.532.4761 (Fax)

conniebeale@att.net

Connie Beale, Inc.

The Regency Hotel
New York, New York

Right: *A wall niche adds detail to the lounge.*
Below: *A lounge area in a contemporary arrangement.*
Opposite: *New lobby seating is set off by open screens.*
Photography: *Phillip Ennis*

Invite a corporate mover and shaker to a "power breakfast" in New York, and he or she will immediately set out for The Regency Hotel. This is the fabled birthplace of the "power breakfast," where major deals are made by many of the world's most influential power brokers, and the "home away from home," where entertainment industry moguls gather their forces on the East Coast. A full 70 percent of guests are repeat customers. How did a $35 million renovation keep this institution at the peak of its form after 30 years of success? For Connie Beale, Inc., the charge from Jonathan Tisch, president and CEO of Loew's Hotels, was to develop an interior design to "contemporize" The Regency yet retain its unique traditions. As Tisch observed, "Connie's vision for the 'new'

Regency gives the hotel a new energy and modern perspective without eliminating the traditional elements that characterize The Regency's reputation." The Regency represents a fascinating blend of Modern architecture and European-inspired traditional interior design that has no peers in New York, so the commission to refurbish virtually every room, including the lobby, restaurant, public areas and guestrooms, and to develop new, one-bedroom suites, required an inspired balance of old and new. The designers introduced a vibrant, contemporary spirit by opening up floor plans, enhancing circulation, raising the level of comfort, and making formal spaces more inviting. On the other hand, they chose contemporary furniture that reflected historic motifs, used mahogany as the hard-

wood of choice for trim and casework, created a timeless color palette of warm neutrals with accents, and specified such fine, traditional materials as mohair, cotton, silk, hardwood flooring, leather and marble, as part of an orchestrated effort to preserve and revitalize the best characteristics of The Regency. As for the power breakfast lobby, the new 540 Park Restaurant features hand-embossed leather, beaded ruby glass sconces and other flourishes to remind them where they are.

Above far left: Bedroom in a new suite. **Below far right:** The contemporary bedroom of the Soho Suite. **Below left:** Guestroom desk and office chair. **Photography:** Thibault Jeanson

Above far left:
Personal touches at the
bedside.
Above right: 540 Park,
home of the "power
breakfast."
Below left: The living
room of the west side
suite.

Connie Beale, Inc.

The Campbell Apartment
Grand Central Terminal
New York, New York

New Yorkers who have never heard of John W. Campbell are enjoying cocktails in his magnificently restored former office. At least that's the impression sought by Mark Grossich, proprietor of The Campbell Apartment, a bar and lounge at Grand Central Terminal. Grossich hired Connie Beale, Inc. to renovate the dormant, 60-foot by 30-foot by 25-foot high space that served the former chairman of Credit Clearing House, a business that was acquired by Dun & Bradstreet, as his private office from 1923 to 1957. Campbell transformed the raw space into a stunning image of a galleried hall in a 13th-century Florentine palazzo with such details as a timber-coffered ceiling, stone fireplace, stained glass windows, architectural millwork, Oriental rugs, antique furniture and even a pipe organ, grand piano and rare books. Campbell and his wife, residents of nearby Westchester County, entertained guests here with concerts, and this spirit of celebration inspired the designers when they installed an elegant mahogany bar, gracious lounge and balcony billiard room that are packed almost every night with latecomers to the Campbells' soirees.

Below left: *A seating area showcasing the cabinetmaker's art.*
Opposite: *The bar, anchoring a Florentine palazzo-like room.*
Photography: *Brad Wilson*

Connie Beale, Inc.

Carnegie Club
New York, New York

Above: *Details of antique cigar humidor.*
Right: *Lounge seating areas featuring antique bookcases.*
Below right: *Bar and mezzanine.*
Photography: *Mick Hales*

Old cities like New York, Boston and Philadelphia have private clubs and other out-of-the-way organizations that function as treasured oases to those fortunate enough to know about them. Connie Beale, Inc. appreciated the possibilities when it was invited to design a jewel-like bar and lounge on two levels for the Carnegie Club in a New York building's unfinished space. The Club's owner, Mark Grossich, commented, "People say it's one of the most beautiful lounges they have ever seen." Impressive as the 2,200-square foot, Edwardian-style watering place is to its patrons, they may not realize that it began with a raw space on a bare concrete slab. Knowing how to make the space come alive, the designers inserted a new mezzanine, created a vocabulary of new and antique furnishings with Edwardian flavor, and devised a twist on the traditional color palette to fit the Carnegie Club into its architectural shell as securely as a tailored suit.

Daroff Design Inc

2300 Ionic Street

Philadelphia

Pennsylvania 19103

215.636.9900

215.636.9627 (Fax)

info@daroffdesign.com

www.daroffdesign.com

Daroff Design Inc

Loews Philadelphia Hotel
Philadelphia, Pennsylvania

On August 1, 1932, Philadelphians peered at their skyline and knew they had never seen anything like the just-completed 36-story Philadelphia Saving Fund Society Building, designed by American architect George Howe and Swiss architect William Lescaze, at 1200 Market Street. The headquarters of PSFS, a slim

tower atop a broad base, was clad in a sleek curtain wall of steel, granite, limestone and glass that exemplified the International Style. Sixty-eight years later, residents of Center City experienced the same sense of wonder when PSFS reopened as the 583-room Loews Philadelphia Hotel, with interior architecture and interior design by Daroff Design Inc., architect of record by Bower Lewis Thrower Architects and historic consultant Powers & Company, Inc.

Above: Main lobby and registration desk.
Left: Approach to lobby.
Right: Seating area in guestroom elevator lobby.
Photography: Peter Paige; cover page: Don Pearse.

Left: *The "must see" lobby bar.*
Directly below: *Banquette seating.*
Below: *Lobby restaurant.*
Bottom: *Lounge accommodations.*
Photography: *Peter Paige*

69

Right: *Concierge level library.*
Below: *Presidential Suite living area.*
Photography: *Don Pearse*

Right: *Presidential suite bedroom.*
Below: *Presidential Suite bathroom.*
Photography: *Don Pearse*

A source of delight to all was the convincing way the office building adapted to modern innkeeping. In the original scheme, retail space on the concourse (subway) level and first floor was separate from public banking functions on the second floor, reached via a multi-story stair and escalator lobby on Market Street, and banking offices on the upper floors, accessible through an elevator lobby off 12th Street. Today, the same areas have new roles in the 628,945-square foot hotel, accommodating back of house facilities, lobby, restaurant and executive offices on the concourse and first floor, such public functions as three ballrooms, prefunction areas, meeting rooms, business center, hospitality suites, fitness center and pool on the 2nd through 5th floors, and guestrooms and suites on the 6th through 32nd floors. The historic 33rd floor boardroom and meeting rooms were retained and refurbished, while the kitchen, two ballrooms and some conference rooms were housed in an 80,000-square foot addition to the building's base. Yet the genius of the Loews Philadelphia is its new hotel interiors, combining restored original details, 1930s Hollywood set design, contemporary design and technology ideas to produce an original aesthetic vision. Who would imagine that the Modernist vocabulary of abstract geometric and organic forms, luxurious natural and

man-made materials and strong colors could yield such an elegantly minimal yet unexpectedly sensual milieu? Everywhere one looks, graceful furniture, patterned carpets and fabrics, dramatic lighting, ornamental metalwork, carved glass and custom art display the dynamism and refinement of the International Style to guests who enjoy access to every amenity and service of the Internet age. No wonder former PSFS chief executive Roger Hilas recently noted, "You can't tell where old ends and new begins in this marvelous place."

Above left: *Millennium Ballroom with Historic Bank vault and view to Historic Headhouse.*
Above right: *Pool with view to spa.*
Top right: *Millennium Ballroom with hangliders.*
Photography: *Don Pearse and Michael Kleinberg*

Di Leonardo
International, Inc.

Hong Kong

852.2.851.7282

852.2.851.7287 (Fax)

London

44. (0) 20.7713.8094

44. (0) 20.7713.8095 (Fax)

World Headquarters:

2350 Post Road

Suite 1

Warwick, Rhode Island 02886.2242

USA

401.732.2900

401.732.5315 (Fax)

info@dileonardo.com

www.dileonardo.com

Offices:

Athens

London

Dallas

Riyadh

Hong Kong

Di Leonardo International, Inc.

Le Merigot Beach Hotel
Santa Monica, California

Left: Outdoor swimming pool and lounge accommodations.
Below: Cezanne, offering French cuisine with Asian influences.
Bottom: Café Promenade for casual California fare.
Photography: Warren Jagger

How do you give guests a taste of the Mediterranean in Southern California? This was the challenge to Di Leonardo International from Le Merigot Hotel, a new, 175-room luxury hotel in downtown Santa Monica that is steps from the beach and minutes from Los Angeles International Airport and the new J. Paul Getty Museum. Forget that the tides remain just beyond reach. The firm drew on the region's sunny climate and spectacular views of the Pacific Ocean and the Santa Monica range to conjure an elegant, sophisticated and comforting mood that echoes the charms of the Cote d'Azur. The interiors immediately surround guests in a distinctive milieu, characterized by artwork reminiscent of Matisse and Dufy, oversized furniture and fixtures with soft clean lines, granite floors, wood-clad columns, Venetiart walls and plush carpets tinted in delicate hues with free-flowing patterns. Yet Le Merigot is also prepared to conduct serious business with fully-equipped guest rooms, state-of-the-art meeting facilities and a rich array of amenities. Each guest room, for example, features fine linen, luxurious upholstered furniture, an ample executive desk, a 25-inch TV and three telephones with data ports. Meeting facilities can satisfy the most demanding planners and attendees with nine meeting rooms—one a spectacular boardroom—and numerous pre-function areas on over 12,000 sq. ft. of flexible space, all brimming with the latest technology. And when work is done, Di Leonardo has fashioned a European Spa, outdoor swimming pool and two seductive choices for fine dining, the Café Promenade, serving casual California fare, and Cezanne, showcasing French cuisine with Asian influences, to let guests plan their own escape to the Cote d'Azur.

Right: Lobby with Mediterranean-style furnishings and color-ways.
Below: Guest room for relaxation and serious business.

Di Leonardo International, Inc.

Ritz-Carlton, Sharm El Sheikh
Sharm El Sheikh, Egypt

Near left: *Lobby Lounge and Library.*
Far left: *Guest room with patio.*
Opposite: *Terraced landscaping overlooking Red Sea.*
Photography: *Warren Jagger*

Diving enthusiasts and adventurous travelers have long known the unique charms of Sharm El Sheikh on Egypt's Southern Sinai Peninsula, overlooking the sapphire blue waters of the Red Sea and the famed Amphora Reefs. To place a 307-room luxury hotel on 100,000 square meters of the Peninsula without disturbing its pristine state, the Ritz-Carlton, Sharm El Sheikh turned to Di Leonardo International for architecture and interior design. As a consequence, the buildings at Africa's first Ritz-Carlton stand only two stories high in stepped forms interspersed with meandering gardens and water works that follow the natural contours of the land, preserving unobstructed views of the sea and the surrounding mountains. Indoors called for a different approach, acknowledging the uncompromising standards of Ritz-Carlton service as well as the growing influence of Western European and Eastern themes on the region's Islamic heritage.

Di Leonardo contrasted traditional Egyptian motifs, which established a timeless sense of place in guest rooms and public spaces, with Western and Eastern themes in recreational facilities, dining and meeting facilities. On land and sea at Sharm El Sheikh, guests revel in a Ritz-Carlton like nowhere else on earth.

Above: *Sunlight-drenched lounge area.*
Right: *Fayrouz Lebanese restaurant.*

Di Leonardo International, Inc.

Phoenix Marriott Hotel
Phoenix, Arizona

Right: Hotel, just 1.5 miles from Sky Harbor airport.
Below: Lobby, with Southwestern motifs and hues.
Photography: Warren Jagger.

Left: Lobby bar with sandstone wall.
Right: Pre-function area.
Below right: Red Rim Bistro.

Business travelers rarely have time during a meeting to see, much less savor, their locale. So capturing a sense of Phoenix as a desert community was one of the major goals set by Di Leonardo International in designing the Phoenix Marriott Hotel. Since this 347-room convention hotel would host many business meetings, being 1.5 miles from Sky Harbor International Airport and close to downtown, the interior design deliberately invokes the warm, dry, Southwestern environment and its Native American culture with a contemporary image that features local sandstone, hammered metal, modern furnishings with an historic flavor, and an earth-toned color palette. Whenever guests emerge from any of 10 meeting rooms, two ballrooms and three executive board rooms on over 18,000 square feet of meeting space, they confront these motifs as they head for their well-appointed, Internet-ready guest rooms, Fitness Center, outdoor pool, gift shop, Lobby Bar or Red Rim Bistro, knowing they are indeed in Phoenix.

Di Leonardo International, Inc.

The Plaza
New York, New York

Guests who register at New York's legendary Plaza Hotel know they are lodging in a shrine to the Gilded Age that opened in 1907 with a design by architect Henry Janeway Hardenbergh. Its builders spared no expense to create the 19-story French chateau, and the rich and famous have been coming ever since, including socialites Mr. and Mrs. Alfred Gwynne Vanderbilt, tenor Enrico Caruso, author F. Scott Fitzgerald and his wife Zelda, and countless heads of state, plus the fictitious Eloise, Kay Thompson's lovable creation. But dealing with a legend is far from simple if you are the design firm retained to restore its aging glories, modernize building systems and provide contemporary services like Internet access.

Di Leonardo International has understood the needs of The Plaza from the start. Even though all 805 guest room and suites, corridors, lobbies, meeting rooms, restaurants and banquet areas are being thoroughly updated for the 21st century, guests never doubt they will encounter Eloise just around the next corner.

Above right: *Meeting room with fireplace.*
Right: *Guest suite for VIP.*
Above: *Detail of guest room.*
Top: *Corridor after Fragonard.*
Photography: *Warren Jagger.*

Dougall Design
Associates, Inc.

35 North Arroyo Parkway

Suite 200

Pasadena

California 91103

626.432.6464

626.432.6460 (Fax)

www.dougalldesign.com

Dougall Design Associates, Inc.

Luxor Hotel and Casino
Las Vegas, Nevada

Below left: *The impressive entrance temple receives guests.*
Opposite: *Guests can dine in a food court like no other.*
Photography: *Berger/Conser*

Far left: *The registration desk displays the Luxor's fine detailing.*
Left: *A favored place to relax is the new night club.*

Nothing stands out forever in the make-believe of Las Vegas, yet one structure still does: The Luxor Hotel and Casino, a sleek, high-tech pyramid rising above the desert. The sense of wonder also lingers indoors, when customers gaze upon the recent renovation by Dougall Design Associates. A restructuring of the public areas has replaced an existing, three-level arrangement involving the casino, attractions and customer services with an exciting and more focused, two-level scheme that guests find easier to navigate. When they come to the new entrance temple, they proceed directly to the lower level casino, registration and night club, or go up to the upper level food court and other attractions, all created in a shimmering, Egyptian-inspired architecture and interior design. Could somebody send for King Tut or Indiana Jones?

Dougall Design Associates, Inc.

The Forum Shops at Caesars
Las Vegas, Nevada

Right: A statue of Venus, Goddess of Beauty, helps pull shoppers through the facility. **Opposite:** Soothing sound and visual drama come from a fountain with dancing waters. **Photography:** Eric Figge, Berger/Conser (fountain)

At the time Dougall Design Associates began Phase I in the development of the Forum Shops at Caesar's Palace in Las Vegas, the assignment seemed quite straightforward: Design a retail venue for the hotel and casino. Now, the Forum Shops are completing Phase III as a legend in the gaming and retailing worlds. Aside from generating some of the highest sales per square foot of gross leasable area, the facility has demonstrated to communities and real estate developers alike the drawing power of a coherent design theme. The designers have taken the ancient Roman architectural orders as the foundation for their concept, establishing a sense of permanence and order that many shopping centers lack. Yet they have also introduced a dynamic element by projecting the passing of the hours from day to night on the painted sky ceilings. When in this Rome, Forum customers don't hesitate to spend like imperial Romans.

Above left: Deep vistas encourage visitors to look far afield. **Above right:** Visual tableaux lend a Baroque air to shopping.

Dougall Design Associates, Inc.   Mandalay Bay Resort and Casino
Las Vegas, Nevada

Right: *The main lobby combines Asian exoticism and European classical order.*
Photography: *Berger/Conser*

Old Tibetan hands and other veteran travelers to Asia may have difficulty pinpointing the inspiration for the casino and public spaces of Mandalay Bay Resort and Casino in Las Vegas, designed by Dougall Design Associates. However, this doesn't prevent guests of the 3,700-room, 60-acre facility from sampling its delights. To avoid the overt use of a specific theme, establish latitude for imaginative work, and distinguish the resort and casino from competitors, the designers drafted a project story line based on the meeting of European cultures with native populations in Asia's tropical zone. The resulting cultural exchanges led to a unique architecture, as the story line goes, that exhibited unique detailing and provided a showcase for Asian and European objets d'art. Whether or not guests understand the design's multi-cultural

Below left: *This restaurant looks East and West.*
Right: *A tromp l'oeil mural enhances a private dining room.*
Bottom: *The casino basks in a tropical glow.*

origins, they are charmed by its distinctive forms, colors, materials and furnishings. The total effect is augmented by a lighting design that casts the casino in a warm, tropical glow and the lagoon in the center of the entertainment lounge under a romantic midnight sky. Mandalay Bay may only exist in Las Vegas, but that's all its guests need to know.

Dougall Design Associates, Inc.

Venetian Resort Casino
Las Vegas, Nevada

Below left: Tiepolo-inspired ceilings crown the opulent interior.
Right: Signage and other details are unabashedly opulent.
Photography: Berger/Conser

When guests spy large-scale replicas of such famous landmarks as the Ca D'Oro and the Campanile looming on the Las Vegas skyline, they know they are approaching the Venetian Resort Casino, which evokes Venice, the fabled Queen of the Adriatic. The Resort's casino was designed by Dougall Design Associates, make no apologies for their opulent homage to such icons as the Danieli Ciga, one of Venice's most famous hotels, or the Doge's Palace, whose façade is replicated as the entrance to the 12,000-square foot casino. Ochre and cream-colored marbles, Tiepolo-inspired frescoed ceilings and plush furnishings seduce the guests—and echo the historic Venetians' own passion for gaming.

Below: The casino honors Venice's famed Danieli Ciga.

Earl Swensson
Associates, Inc.

2100 West End Avenue

Suite 1200

Nashville

Tennessee 37203

615.329.9445

615.329.0046 (Fax)

www.esarch.com

info@esarch.com

Earl Swensson
Associates, Inc.

The Delta at Opryland Hotel
Nashville, Tennessee

Right: The Old Hickory
Steakhouse in the Delta.
Below: Restaurant
entrance with fountain.
Photography: Michael
Lewis (Presidential
Suite), Jonathan Hillyer

Above: *Presidential Suite bedroom*
Below: *Foyer of Presidential Suite.*

Opryland Hotel Nashville is the largest hotel and convention center under one roof in the world. It features 2,884 rooms, 9 acres of indoor gardens and 600,000 square feet of state-of-the-art convention facilities. But it didn't start out that way. Earl Swensson Associates designed the original hotel of 600 rooms, as well as the three additions to the hotel, bringing it to its current size.

The latest expansion produced the Delta, a 4.5-acre indoor garden under a sprawling glass roof featuring a quarter-mile-long river with boats running through it.

The Delta also features the Old Hickory Steakhouse housed in an antebellum style mansion on top of a mountain with cascading waterfalls. The black and white stone flooring, fluted columns, leaded glass, fountain and Empire furniture promise a memorable dining experience. The Delta section also features the 5,100 square foot Presidential Suite where every design detail was meant to delight guests. Advanced communication systems are art-fully integrated into a Victorian-style environment with a fireplace, baby grand piano,

whirlpool and large-screen television. The design details of the Opryland Hotel will make a permanent impression on its guests.

Earl Swensson Associates, Inc.

The Broadmoor Golf Clubhouse
Colorado Springs, Colorado

With ruggedly handsome architecture and commanding views of the Rocky Mountains, The Broadmoor, in Colorado Springs, holds a special place in the hearts of guests who have been coming since 1918. Many would insist that the best change for The Broadmoor would be no change at all. Happily, the attractive new, 80,000-square foot Golf Clubhouse, designed by Earl Swensson Associates, satisfies both a pressing need for modern facilities and a respect for tradition. The structure functions as golf lockers, pro shop, fitness area, pool, spa, restaurant and meeting rooms through a scheme that provides up-to-date guest services, establishes clear access to related activities, existing accommodations and the roadside, captures outdoor views and natural light, and relates to the historic property. All this may seem secondary to patrons, for whom the warm, traditional design, featuring interiors graced by fine wood and upholstered furniture, wool Axminster carpet, cherry wood, accents of pecan, sandstone and marble, plus etched, golf-themed dining room windows relocated from the existing clubhouse, testifies that the old Broadmoor thrives in the gracious new Golf Clubhouse.

Above: *Clubhouse exterior.*
Below left: *Dining room with golf-themed windows.*
Photography: *Jonathan Hillyer*

Right: Pool and spa.
Below: Cocktail lounge.

93

Earl Swensson
Associates, Inc.

The Hotel Hershey
Hershey, Pennsylvania

Opposite above: New elevator lobby.
Opposite: Fountain lobby lounge.
Above: Milton S. Hershey Suite.
Below: Typical guestroom.
Photography: Sam Todd Dyess

Call it a very big sweet tooth, but Americans love to visit the quaint Pennsylvania town whose star attraction is the chocolate factory founded by Milton S. Hershey in 1903. In providing planning and design services to the popular Hotel Hershey, Earl Swensson Associates created the Milton S. Hershey Suite, made existing guestrooms ADA compliant, and upgraded utility infrastructure for telecommunications, plumbing, electrical and fire protection. The visual impact, kept low-key to enhance the existing rustic Mediterranean theme, was considerable nonetheless. The Milton Hershey Suite, for example, required the consolidation of five existing guestrooms to create a larger open space. Sprinklers were installed in guestroom corridors without destroying the original barrel vault ceilings. Guestrooms received crown moldings, drywall ceilings, custom draperies, wood blinds, wall sconces at entries, travertine bathroom floors and shower surrounds. Elevator lobbies were carved from adjacent guestrooms and outfitted with stone floors, pendant lighting fixtures and occasional furniture to bring Mediterranean aesthetics to a later addition that lacked visual distinction. The result is a sweeter stay for families touring a town in America where the streetlights look like Hershey's Kisses®.

Earl Swensson Associates, Inc.

The Aspen Institute
Queenstown, Maryland

Can a house be more than a home? For the Aspen Institute, it could be a conference center, and Earl Swensson Associates was retained to make this vision possible. The result is the Aspen Institute's Aspen Wye River Conference Center in Queenstown, Maryland, a unique facility that plays host to many of the Institute's seminars and policy programs. It is through these programs that the Institute fosters enlightened, morally responsible leadership and convenes leaders and policy makers to address the foremost challenges of the new century. In addition, this 35,000-square foot, four-story center hosts many private meetings throughout the year. Still, the renovated and expanded Center deliberately emphasizes the reassuring stability of its Georgian-style layout, a central stair hall flanked by wings, and its residential, early American-style interiors. Such domestic touches as a fireplace, grand piano, indoor plants and wicker furniture in the lounges, guestrooms, dining room and fitness center are surely appreciated when people emerge from intense sessions in the state-of-the-art multi-media conference facilities to find themselves "at home."

Above: Center staircase.
Upper right: Conference room.
Right: Main lobby lounge.
Lower right: Sun room.
Photography: Otto Baitz

Elness Swenson Graham Architects Inc.

700 Third Street South

Minneapolis, Minnesota 55415

612.339.5508   Minneapolis

612.339.5382 (Fax)   Dallas

www.esgarch.com   Phoenix

Elness Swenson Graham Architects Inc.

Miccosukee Resort and Convention Center
Miami, Florida

Alligator wrestling is no longer the only exciting pastime in the Everglades. Now that Florida's Miccosukee Tribe of Indians has developed the Miccosukee Resort and Convention Center some 20 miles west of the Miami airport, a new kind of action is taking place. Designed by Elness Swenson Graham Architects Inc. with ICI Design International as interior design consultant for Kraus-Anderson Construction Company, as part of a design build team serving the Miccosukee Tribe, the Resort joins 271,500 square feet of new space to the existing Miccosukee Bingo and Gaming Hall. Included in the addition are a 302-room hotel, three restaurants, an 11,000-square foot ballroom, a 22,000-square foot Class 2 gaming area, a 7,000-square foot child care/teen center and a health club. The project is distinctive in more ways than one. Though the Miccosukee tribal logo and decorative geometric patterns are discreetly revealed in

Above: The striking exterior appeals to the mostly Latino clientele. **Left:** The festive buffet restaurant, one of three at the Resort. **Photography:** C.J. Walker.

Above right: The dramatic two-story high main entry lobby sets the mood.
Right: An inviting and well-appointed lobby bar lets customers relax.

floors and wallcoverings, the overall design consciously revels in vivid colors, deep recesses, curvilinear ceilings, assymmetrical geometric forms and an absence of classical ornamentation—all motifs with visual counterparts in South America, Mexico and Miami Beach—to appeal directly to the mostly Latino clientele. It goes without saying that the space respects the special needs of gaming facilities. The first floor gaming area, for example, is surrounded by amenities that welcome the outside walls, natural light and views it cannot use; a major circulation spine and series of low walls let children enjoy full access to amenities without walking through gaming areas; and a spectacular, two-story high main entry lobby generates the kind of drama that sets the stage for the gaming activities inside. The Everglades are not just for the alligators any more.

Above: *The 22,000-square foot gaming floor offers plenty of action.*
Right: *Formal dining has its place at the Resort's specialty restaurant.*

Above: This guest suite living room offers glamour at a personal level.

Elness Swenson Graham Architects Inc.

Imation Discovery Technology Center Cafeteria
Oakdale, Minnesota

Right: The Rotunda is Imation's main entry.
Below: A view of the Cafeteria's dynamic form.
Photography: Dana Wheelock

If modern life is a work in progress, research and development (R&D) centers are apt symbols of our time, keeping their laboratories and offices open, flexible and neutral for endless modifications. Yet because scientists, technicians and other R&D personnel do enjoy visually stimulating environments and frequently hold productive "brainstorming" sessions in them, projects like Imation's Discovery Technology Center in Oakdale, Minnesota, designed by Elness Swenson Graham Architects Inc., include attractive support facilities for relaxation and socializing. The 438,000-square foot Center serving Imation Enterprises, a $2 billion, 9,000-employee spin-off of 3M that produces goods and services for information and image management, consists of three, four-story high R&D/office modules linked by support "knuckles" where employees can find various services and amenities. It's in the central customer and scientist support module, the focal point of the Center, where the Cafeteria can be found, along with a rotunda, library, conference rooms and training facility. The Cafeteria is in constant use as the visual, social and functional centerpiece of the Imation Corporate Campus, a satisfying respite from the demands of work, and a forum for meetings and presentations that happens to feed 1800 high-tech people every working day. In fact, its dynamic space, sweeping views and exposed truss ceiling have become an integral part of Imation's interactive network.

Right: *The curving exterior of the Cafeteria contrasts with the rectilinear R&D/office modules.*

Elness Swenson Graham Architects Inc.

Fortune Bay Resort Casino, Lake Vermillion Tower, Minnesota

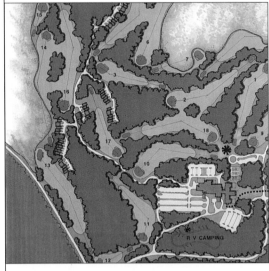

Casinos normally transport customers to a wondrous, make-believe realm where the outside world is invisible, but Fortune Bay Resort Casino on Lake Vermillion in Tower, Minnesota, gazes upon a magnificent forest that is hard to ignore. Given this context, Elness Swenson Graham Architects Inc. drafted a master plan to develop the existing bingo hall and casino into a year-round resort and conference center that would acknowledge the landscape and thrive as a resort independently of gaming. The first phase of the project saw the construction of 18,000 square feet of gaming area and a night club within the existing casino, as well as an adjoining, 118-room hotel, a 225-seat buffet restaurant, conference facilities, an indoor swimming pool and water treatment facilities. Fortune Bay differs from other Minnesota casinos in yet another visible way. Evoking a great north woods lodge, it offers guests a main lobby, conference center, indoor recreational facilities and guestrooms that national park guests would love.

Top: Fortune Bay's master plan.
Above: Indoor swimming pool.
Right: Main lobby with 35-foot fireplace.
Photography: Stuart Lorenz.

Floss Barber, Inc.

Architects Building

Penthouse

117 South 17th Street

Philadelphia, Pennsylvania 19103

215.557.0700

215.557.6700 (Fax)

floss@flossbarber.com

flossbarber.com

Floss Barber, Inc.

Rococo
Philadelphia, Pennsylvania

Intimate dining in a Neoclassical grand hall at Philadelphia's Corn Exchange Building of 1857 is not an oxymoron, as awed young Philadelphians have happily discovered at Rococo. The 120-seat, 7,500-square foot restaurant on two levels designed for chef Al Paris and partner Philippe Daouphars by Floss Barber, Inc. acknowledges its extraordinary surroundings without being overwhelmed by them. What makes the solution so successful is its ability to simultaneously embrace the monumental space and scale itself down in measured steps to the size of a table for two. All this happens while the interior casts a spell made possible by combining the "masculine" qualities of the 19th century architectural orders with more "feminine" qualities from late 20th century interior design, including the low, serpentine partitions in the main dining room, the sprawling, baroque bar backed by tall, slender mirrors, the color scheme of gold leaf, cobalt blue and earth tones, the enormous urns standing on either side of the main entrance, the curving staircase ascending to an upper level cigar lounge, the wood paneled, floor-to-ceiling wine wall, and the open kitchen at the back. Thus, customers are always aware of Rococo's vast dining room as a magnificent background, but they find their attention drawn to the colorful freestanding objects in the middle ground, such as the bar, wine wall or urns, whenever they look up from wherever they are seated. The memorable quality of the interior even has "uptown lawyers" three-deep at the bar gazing in wonder.

Above: Wine wall adds sensuality to Neoclassicism.
Right: Serpentine bar is happy hour oasis for young.
Opposite: Graceful stairway to cigar lounge.
Photography: Tom Crane, Catherine Tigue

Floss Barber, Inc.

Sansom Street Oyster House
Philadelphia, Pennsylvania

Above: *Clerestory window opens up corner space.*
Left: *Dark wainscoting plays off bright walls.*
Below left: *Accent tiles for existing tile floor.*
Opposite: *Oyster bar anchors the dining rooms.*
Photography: *John Carlano*

"If it ain't broke, don't fix it." Patrons of Philadelphia's Sansom Street Oyster House were understandly concerned when their 140-seat, 2,400-square foot bastion of fresh, simply prepared and fairly priced seafood closed for four weeks of remodeling by Floss Barber, Inc. The oyster house was started in 1975 by restaurateur David Mink as a descendent of the legendary Kelly's, an institution founded by Mary and "Pa" Kelly in 1901, purchased by Mink's father Sam in 1947, and managed by Mink until it was sold in the 1970s. Like many another legend, of course, what existed was not quite what regulars remembered. Superb as the seafood was, featuring such glories as the oyster bar's "seafood plateau," the dining rooms were dark, closed off and dreary. Juggling a modest budget and tight timetable with Mink's desire to rejuvenate the space, the designers enlarged the granite-topped oyster bar, opened up the dining areas by taking down walls, punched out cafe windows to let daylight in, repainted walls lime green and terra-cotta red, and saved and refurbished everything else. The restaurant's recent reopening drew raves from critics and customers who promptly reclaimed "their" oyster house.

Floss Barber, Inc.

Sheraton
Rittenhouse Square Hotel
Philadelphia, Pennsylvania

Right: "Green" fabrics and finishes seen close up.
Below: Lobby with 40-foot high bamboo garden.
Photography: Tom Crane, Barry Halkin, Bill Bettencourt, The Philadelphia Inquirer

Above right: Leaf medallions of recycled glass.
Right: Elegant bar in one of four restaurants.

A 40-foot high bamboo garden in the lobby is your first hint of the uniquely attractive and healthy environment at Philadelphia's recently opened, 139-room Sheraton Rittenhouse Square Hotel, designed by Floss Barber, Inc. Not only does Sheraton's first environmentally responsible or "green" hotel offer guests 400-square foot, Internet-linked guestrooms, seven meeting rooms, a business services center, a fitness center, four restaurants and lounges. It also minimizes its environmental impact and optimizes its living conditions through fresh, filtered air in guestrooms 24 hours a day, 100 percent organic cotton bedding and drapery, beds of cotton and wool free of toxic bleaches or dyes, furniture of wood from managed forests with a rugged, catalytic finish, toxic-free paint, wallpaper, carpeting and fabrics, environmentally safe laundry and cleaning products, and recycled building materials. As for the lobby's bamboo garden, it oxygenates the air where people continually congregate, so the uplift you feel there is more than psychological.

Floss Barber, Inc.

Sands Hotel & Casino
Atlantic City, Jew Jersey

What the Sands Hotel & Casino in Las Vegas wanted from Floss Barber, Inc. could not be simpler or more enigmatic: make the "high roller" suites on its top two floors "lavish," working from corridors to exterior walls and from slab to slab. The designers interpreted "lavish" to mean "glamorous," and developed striking design concepts for the suites using New York apartments of the Art Deco age and Hollywood homes of the Art Moderne era as role models. Being on the uppermost floors had its advantages because the penthouse ceiling could readily accommodate such creative design elements as domes, barrel vaults and coffers, and duplexes could be created by breaking through the floor slab. Imaginative floor plans, sections and elevations provided an ideal foundation for clean-lined furniture based on traditional forms and complementary furnishings, all keyed to natural color palettes with metallic accents fit for a president, king or high roller.

Top: A superbly tailored living room.
Above: Raising the ceiling highlights a grand salon.
Right: A bedroom of quiet luxury.
Photography: John Woodin

Fugleberg Koch

2555 Temple Trail
Winter Park
Florida 32789
800.393.0595
407.628.1057 (Fax)
www.fuglebergkoch.com

Fugleberg Koch

Club Hotel by Doubletree
Orlando, Florida

Below: Exterior with bold graphics and 20-foot pineapple.
Photography: Michael Lowry Photography, Inc. and Ron Kunzman Photography, Inc.

Can life begin again if you are the latest owner of a newly flagged but conventional, 1970s-style hotel in Orlando that is a short distance from Walt Disney World Resort, yet in dire need of a facelift? Acknowledging the 245-room Club Hotel by Doubletree's moderate budget and need for uninterrupted opera-

tions, Fugleberg Koch opened up the lobby/bar area to provide a view to the pool deck, relocated the restaurant to introduce an income-producing business office and conference room, varied the mix of guestrooms by adding club suites and children's suites, and created a "Tropical Magic" theme

to transform the facility inside and out. The theme had an immediate impact on the hotel's image. On the façade, the architects drew attention with a bold color palette, oversized tropical fruit ornaments, story-high metal cutouts, theatrical lighting and tropical landscaping. Inside, they used bold

geometries, whimsical colors, columns that resemble palm trees, ceilings showing coffers and blue skies, and stylish furnishings that captured guests' imagination. In one bold stroke, the Club Hotel by Doubletree has repositioned itself to compete with some of the entertainment industry's savvi-

est operators—and to have a visually exuberant good time doing so.

Above: *Festive colors draw guests to the lobby/bar.*
Right: *A typical kids suite stylish appointments.*

Fugleberg Koch

Grand Country Square
Branson, Missouri

Left: Signage at the Grand Country Market.
Opposite: *The 64-foot long banjo that country western stars sign.*
Photography: *Michael Lowry Photography, Inc.*

Left: *The main entrance to the restaurant & entertainment.*
Below left: *A view of the water park.*
Below right: *Thematic design at the retail store.*

It could be the prospect of seeing beloved music stars in distinctive venues of their own choosing that draws families to Branson, Missouri, an entertainment mecca with a Country & Western soul. It could be the crowd-pleasing hospitality. It could be the relaxed, informal style. Whatever the cause, the public arrives by carload and busload, and the owner of Grand Country Square, a three-acre, 111,200-square foot hotel and retail complex, sought to win them over by retaining Fugleberg

Koch to remodel the property. The designers wrote a fictional storyline about "Grandpa and Grandma Grand's travels to the New Frontier" that helped them assign a role in the adventure to each of the buildings in the complex, including a Family Entertainment Center, themed restaurant and retail store, Live Show Performance Theater and 22,000-square foot water park. As a result, occupancy and earnings have shot up and such features as a 64-foot long banjo and 42-foot long fiddle have

become instant icons, In fact, stars like Dale Evans, The Osmonds, The Oakridge Boys and Roy Clark have started a new tradition by signing the banjo when they come to Branson. It's not your everyday design, that's for sure.

Fugleberg Koch

Charles Towne at Park Central
Orlando, Florida

Right: Fieldhouse accommodations are inviting.
Below: The sports pub is for residents only.
Photography: Robert Starling Photography, Inc.

Right: *A view of the Key West-style architecture.*
Below right: *The field-house builds community spirit.*

Marriage and children are coming later in the lives of young Americans, freeing many to enjoy a prolonged, adolescent lifestyle that has been glamorized in such popular TV programs as Friends, Seinfeld and Beverly Hills 90210. A good example of the resort-like housing being developed for active "Gen Xers" is Charles Towne at Park Central, located between downtown Orlando and its famous attractions, which Fugleberg Koch recently designed for young corporate executives and entertainment industry employees. The 413-unit development, designed in the Key West vernacular, offers an amenity package that includes a community "fieldhouse" with group sports facilities and a residents-only sports pub. Yet costs were not excessive due to such creative design techniques as the third-floor "loft" apartments occupying unused second-floor attic space, so 60 percent of the project's units could have premium vaulted ceilings. While life at Charles Towne may not resemble a Friends episode, occupancy is high, turnover low and residents are staying tuned.

Fugleberg Koch

Hilton Grande Vacations
Orlando and Miami, Florida

Top: Exterior of Orlando
structure.
Top right: *Typical
Orlando unit.*
Above: *South Beach Art
Deco façade.*
Right: *Restored lobby
in South Beach.*
Photography: *Michael
Lowry Photography, Inc.*

Competition for the time-
share market may up the
ante in the hospitality
industry, but it also makes
design more critical than
ever. For this reason,
Hilton Grande Vacations,
the timeshare arm of
Hilton Corporation, has
championed good design
in entrusting Fugleberg
Koch with two Florida
developments, a 26-unit
renovation in chic South
Beach and a new, 48-unit-
per-building complex in
burgeoning Orlando. An
aging South Beach Art
Deco apartment building
was transformed into the
McAlpin Hotel by restor-
ing the lobby to its original condition and strip-
ping the three-story-plus-
penthouse structure to its
historical shell to create
four stories of one- and
two-bedroom units. The
Orlando project, with
nine of ten buildings
completed to date,
reduced costs without
diminishing market
appeal in its Bermuda-
inspired, horseshoe-
shaped form by exploiting
systematized floor plans
and modular design, stan-
dardized building compo-
nents and straightforward
massing to deliver quality
accommodations at $100
per square foot. Either
way, Hilton Grande
Vacations has attractive
design options for making
Florida your seasonal
address.

Gensler

Arlington	London
Atlanta	Los Angeles
Baltimore	New Jersey
Boston	New York
Charlotte	Newport Beach
Chicago	San Francisco
Dallas	San Jose
Denver	San Ramon
Detroit	Seattle
Hong Kong	Tokyo
Houston	Washington, DC
LaCrosse	www.gensler.com

Gensler

Hotel Palomar
San Francisco, California

"Small is beautiful" appeals to hotel guests who appreciate the warmth, personal attention and idiosyncratic nature of small establishments. Guided by this sentiment, San Francisco's Hotel Palomar has made a virtue of its modest, 198-room size in a design by Gensler and Cheryl Rowley Design. The 125,000-square foot hotel resembles an exquisite Parisian private club or residence in the Art Deco era, paying homage to such talented individuals as Emile-Jacques Ruhlmann in its guest rooms, living room, meeting facilities, fitness center, restaurant and bar. At the same time, it overcomes such physical obstacles as minimum space at street level, low ceiling heights and windowless spaces—the price for converting a turn-of-the-century poured concrete office building to retailing and hospitality—by placing a dramatic entrance at street level to entice guests to the lobby on the fifth floor, introducing cove lighting to suggest greater elevation, and turning walls into "light screens" to simulate natural light. Such carefully chosen furnishings as exotic veneers, transitional furniture, parquet floors, rich, dark colors and bronze decorative lighting fixtures provided a taste of Paris, complementing such modern services as Internet connections in every guest room—discreetly housed in the armoire, of course.

Above left: The Parisian-style restaurant.
Above: Front desk furnishings evoke Ruhlmann.
Photography: *David Phelps*

Above right: *A smartly appointed guestroom.*
Right: *Idiosyncratic details in the lobby.*

Gensler

Fairmont Hotel San Francisco
San Francisco, California

Right: *A mezzanine view of the lobby.*
Photography: *Sherman Takata*

Revered as one of San Francisco's reigning dowagers, the Fairmont Hotel, designed by the Reid Brothers from 1902-1906, registered guests prominent in business, politics, sports and entertainment from the moment it opened on Nob Hill in 1910. Entrusted to Gensler, in collaboration with Wilson & Associates and Virginia Ball Desiges, Inc., for the historic renovation and an upgrading of its bathrooms and other facilities, the 596-room, 225,000-square foot landmark recently emerged in all its historic splendor. The lack of discernable changes testifies to the diligence of the designers, who sought to protect the historic fabric, reverse the effects of alterations, maintain and clarify historic room layouts, and incorporate state-of-the-art building technologies and services. What began as a feasibility report for renovation expanded to include space planning studies, architectural design services and a textbook-style historic preservation, including the uncovering of hidden domes, a careful reworking of color schemes old and new, the installation of new furnishings reminiscent of the 1900s, and a lighting design that added natural light by reopening clerestory windows in the main lobby. Guests coming to the public areas, guestrooms, spa, meeting and banquet facilities, restaurants and bars know the Fairmont reigns again on its Nob Hill throne.

Left: *A stately lounge and its restored dome.*
Above: *A close-up of the railing's fine ironwork.*
Opposite: *The main historic lobby as arriving guests see it.*

Gensler

The Regent Beverly Wilshire
Beverly Hills, California

In 1928, The Regent Beverly Wilshire Hotel towered over the intersection of Rodeo Drive and Wilshire Boulevard as one of the tallest and most glamorous structures in the early days of the motion picture business, and became an instant destination for the stars. The stars came, sure enough—Barbara Hutton, Cary Grant, Dashiel Hammett (who wrote "The Thin Man" series there), Elvis Presley, Warren Beatty, John Lennon, Al Pacino, Michael Douglas and Elton John among others—and have kept coming, along with such dignitaries as the Emperor Hirohito, the Dalai Lama, the Aga Kahn and most of Great Britain's Royal Family. However, even show business legends can benefit from facelifts, so the hotel's owners launched a major renovation in 1996 by retaining Gensler for architecture services and Hirsch Bedner Associates for interior design. The project was as carefully staged as an opening night to refurbish the hotel's two sections, the Wilshire wing, built in 1928, and the Beverly wing, built in 1971, with as little interruption as possible to guests and operations.

Top: A one bedroom suite.
Above: A swimming pool area.
Left: The bar at lobby lounge restaurant.
Opposite: A seating area in the dining room.
Photography: Robert Miller

Right: *A typical deluxe guestroom.*
Below: *The Presidential Suite living room.*
Bottom: *Formal dining in the Presidential Suite.*

Though the bulk of the project involved new furniture, plumbing, HVAC risers and wall-coverings, carpet and other finishes for the guestrooms in the Wilshire wing and those on floors 3-6 of the Beverly wing, the upper part of the Beverly wing, floors 7-14, required demolition to convert them from residential apartments to 120 new guestrooms and a 3500-square foot Presidential Suite on the 14th floor. Not only did everything proceed smoothly in the guestrooms, along with new finishes and fabrics for the two main dining rooms and the lobby entry sequence, the hotel has emerged to enjoy one of its most successful years to date, a box office boffo its guests can appreciate.

The Gettys Group, Inc.

One East Erie Street

Chicago

Illinois 60611

312.836.1111

312.836.1133 (Fax)

www.gettys.com

The Gettys Group, Inc.

Radisson Hotel New York East Side
New York, New York

Below left: *This guest living room setting has a gracious and welcoming residential aura.*
Below: *Sophisticated furnishings help reposition the hotel in a higher market segment.*
Photography: *David Clifton Photography.*

When a recent poll asked New Yorkers where they might meet someone if they forgot to name a specific place, they overwhelmingly chose Grand Central Terminal, a beloved landmark in Manhattan's East Side. It's the centerpiece of a thriving neighborhood of offices, shops, restaurants, apartments and some of the city's liveliest hotels, including the newly renovated Radisson Hotel New York East Side, designed by The Gettys Group. The Radisson's facelift is a successful story about how designers can help hoteliers stand out from the crowd and prosper in a highly competitive market. Management knew that rival hotels were being refurbished and upgraded just steps away. To reposition the 700-plus-room facility for increased visibility, style and perceived quality, the new design has introduced a fresh, contemporary ambiance that looks decidedly upmarket for Radisson. The modern furnishings and finishes have been carefully chosen because they are sleek, sophisticated and durable without being expensive. For the finishing touch, classic black-and-white photographs portraying quintessential images of Gotham let guests proudly say: I'll take Manhattan.

Above: Superbly composed guestrooms have emerged from highly irregular existing floor plans.
Right: A rendering depicts the future main lobby as a chic and distinctive gathering place.

131

The Gettys Group, Inc.

Sheraton Atlanta
Atlanta, Georgia

Left: This lounge setting unites past and present in the new hotel environment.
Below left: Redesigned exterior with open-air canopy.
Bottom: The bar combines Atlanta's beloved classicism with the whimsical spirit of modern life.
Photography: David Clifton Photography.

The proud, ambitious city where Margaret Mitchell wrote Gone with the Wind manages to be both progressive and traditional, and the newly updated, 750-room Sheraton Atlanta, designed by The Gettys Group, illustrates its contemporary spirit. A new porte-cochere and a refreshed exterior complement remodeled public spaces and guest-rooms, attracting business and leisure travelers alike. The design's stunning colors, unusual geometric and amorphous shapes, contrasting textures and playful architectural details immerse guests in an unforgettable setting that should beguile Atlanta well into the new Millennium.

The Gettys Group, Inc.

Marriott New York East Side
New York, New York

Right: *A modern interior design enlarges the perceived size of the guestroom.*
Photography: *David Clifton Photography.*

Left: *Furnishings provide thoughtful details for business and leisure travelers.*

While the size of the American home has risen past 1800 square feet, the size of the American household has fallen to just slightly over two persons. But don't expect any sympathy from citizens of dense cities like New York, where undersized spaces and oversized rents are a way of life. When the Marriott New York East Side recently asked The Gettys Group to help re-introduce its historic property to the city's competitive market by renovating its small, dark existing guestrooms, the designers decided to make these spaces feel more generous and elegantly appointed than ever before. Their solution incorporates clean, sophisticated and modern furnishings, materials and artwork plus a richly hued color palette. Higher room rates and occupancy show that quality has triumphed over quantity once again on New York's East Side.

133

The Gettys Group, Inc.

Wyndham Oak Brook
Oak Brook, Illinois

Progress American-style can turn a charming rural community of farms, horse stables and forests into an affluent suburb of homes, shopping centers and office parks. The consequences are handsomely displayed in the renovation of the 160-room Wyndham Oak Brook Hotel, by The Gettys Group. The 35-year-old property, just outside Chicago, was originally a social destination in a "country club" environment where established families celebrated the marriages of their sons and daughters as well as other special events. Having outlasted its bucolic surroundings and encountered a host of younger rivals, the hotel recently embarked on a refurbishment and modernization that targeted the needs of local families and business people from the area's many corporate headquarters. The fast-track project resulted in a gracious design for a moderate budget. Improvements are apparent wherever guests view the interiors, in which spaces flow better, functions are served by well-equipped

Opposite: *The lobby welcomes guests with a fireplace and lobby bar and lounge*
Above: *A warm, inviting atmosphere pervades the lobby bar.*
Top: *Typical lounge settings evoke a country estate milieu.*
Photography: *Jon Miller ©, Hedrich-Blessing, Ltd.*

facilities, and materials and furnishings power-fully evoke the area's rural heritage. Bridal parties and executive conferences readily identify with the new, country estate imagery of oak columns, beams and paneling, marble floors, contemporary furnishings inspired by 18th and 19th century styles, fine rugs and wallcoverings, a stone-lined fireplace and hand-screened murals depicting early America. Once again, the hotel is "the" place to be in Oak Brook.

Top: *Business travelers like guestrooms set up for work.*
Above left: *A more residential guestroom caters to bridal parties.*
Above right: *Guest bath rooms offer understated elegance.*

Haverson Architecture and Design, PC

63 Church Street

Greenwich

Connecticut 06830

203.629.8300

203.629.8399 (Fax)

www.haversonarchitecture.com

Haverson Architecture and Design, PC

Harley-Davidson Cafe
Las Vegas, Nevada

Right: *The Café as seen from the Strip.*
Below: *Main dining room and chain link flag.*
Photography: *Paul Warchol*

You can almost hear a potato-potato-potato rumble from the 28-foot tall Heritage Softail breaking through the wall of the Harley-Davidson Cafe once you spy the giant motorcycle on the legendary Strip in Las Vegas. It's just one reason business has been brisk at the 400-seat Café. To translate the famed brand into a successful restaurant, Haverson Architecture and Design, PC incorporated the current line of "bikes" and bike parts, historic artifacts, and authentic colors and materials into a dynamic, multi-level space for dining, bar, band stand, retail shop and back-of-house functions. Throw in a moving assembly line of new models, a 25-foot x 40-foot American flag of chain link and a ceiling road map of Route 66 and it's easy to see why dining at the Café is like riding a Harley—with good food to boot.

Left: A view of multi-level dining areas.
Right: Route 66 Bar with overhead map of legendary Harley Davidson road.

Above: Hand crafted Harley Davidson eagle above dining area.
Right: Gift shop with apparel and other gear.

Haverson Architecture and Design, PC

Sport Plus at New Roc City
New Rochelle, New York

To shop or be entertained? Americans appear to want both, and New Rochelle's 450,000-square foot New Roc City retail complex is paired with a 150,000-square foot Sports Plus Family Entertainment Center, both designed by Haverson Architecture and Design, PC, to give customers what they want. New Roc City consists of two separate principal structures. A seven-story parking garage with an office building at the east end and a 100-room, all-suite hotel at the west end forms the northern part, while a three-level retail building covering the equivalent of two city blocks represents the southern part. The elevations of the two structures are designed to be friendly and accessible by recalling an early 20th century urban street with 19 facades resembling such familiar building types as a firehouse, a 19th century cast-iron building and a Neoclassical municipal building. Visitors who cross the pedestrian bridge between the two structures, which playfully mimics a suspension bridge, find themselves in an atrium of storefronts with playful and open facades that entice people to stay and shop. Prominent within the atrium is the Space Shot tower, which propels people vertically, one of the featured activities of Sports Plus, the largest of New Roc City's attractions. Eager for an NHL-type skating rink, a Central Park Skating Pond, an adventure ride, an arcade with midway games, a laser tag game, a playground with carousels, a capsule-based ride, a billiard room or various food and beverage concessions? There's enough here to keep individuals and groups happily engrossed without having to choose between shopping or entertainment.

Above: Streetscape of New Roc City facades. *Below left:* Third level of the Atrium. *Below right:* Pedestrian bridge over New Street. *Photography:* Paul Warchol.

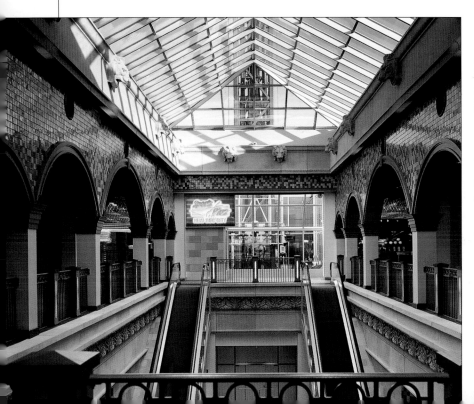

Right: *The Reunion Cafe at Sports Plus.*
Far right: *Billiard tables at The Cue.*

Above: *National Hockey League rink with paintings of athletes on walls.*

Haverson Architecture and Design, PC

Smith & Wollensky at Marina City
Chicago, Illinois

The City with the Big Shoulders likes its steakhouses USDA Choice. So restaurateur Alan Stillman of the New York Restaurant Group commissioned Haverson Architecture and Design, PC, to create a Chicago branch of his popular Smith & Wollensky at Chicago's Marina City that could simultaneously capture the Old World character of Manhattan's 1977 flagship restaurant and acknowledge the feisty spirit of the Windy City. Placing the 26,000-square foot, 400-seat establishment at the base of architect Bertrand Goldberg's landmark twin, 60-story residential towers added yet another goal—the approval of the City Planning Board. The restaurant skillfully accounts for these concerns while providing an appetizing environment for serious carnivores. Space is divided among three settings overlooking the Chicago River, including a pavilion restaurant on Marina City's plaza and the Smith & Wollensky Restaurant and Wollensky's Grill just below. Rooms that flow into one another share such turn-of-the-century elements as maple wainscoting, marble-banded chair rails, buttery-painted walls, flush tile ceilings and exposed sprinklers, along with the restaurant's signature antique collection of bulls, bears and eagles, framed paintings, sports artifacts, nautical gear and Chicago World's Fair memorabilia. Chicagoans like it enough to visit its small retail shop, Mrs. Wollensky's Butchery, and take a "slice" home.

Above: *The Marina City location.*
Below left: *The bar at Wollensky's Grill.*
Below: *Cabinetry for the wine collection.*
Opposite: *Pavilion dining room and shop.*
Opposite below: *River view at the Grill.*
Photography: *Paul Warchol.*

Haverson Architecture and Design, PC

Motown Cafe at the New York New York Hotel & Casino Las Vegas, Nevada

A host or hostess wearing classic Motown performance apparel at the lobby rotunda lets you know that you can expect more than good food in the Motown Cafe at the New York New York Hotel & Casino in Las Vegas, designed by Haverson Architecture and Design, PC. Patrons who visit the Twenty Grand main dining room, the Stairway to Success to the mezzanine and Twenty Grand Bar, Radio Motown DJ/VJ booth, Marvin Gaye Lounge and Shop Around retail store cannot help being swept into the defining moments in the life of Motown artists. Not only are accommodations modeled along actual venues visited by such groups as The Supremes, The Temptations, Stevie Wonder and The Four Tops, there are also dioramas with statues of the stars depicting the events. Supporting the Café's dazzling vision is a well planned, 28,000-square foot, 650-seat space that blends seductive forms with shimmering materials to convince happy customers to "Reach Out, I'll Be There."

Above left: Diana Ross private dining area.
Top left: Private dining area.
Upper right: Twenty Grand room.
Lower right: Entry/Stairway to Success.
Top right: Exterior marquis.
Photography: Paul Warchol.

Hirsch Bedner Associates

3216 Nebraska Avenue

Santa Monica, California 90404

310.829.9087

310.453.1182 (Fax)

www.hbadesign.com

Atlanta

Hong Kong

London

Los Angeles

San Francisco

Singapore

Hirsch Bedner Associates

Pan Pacific Yokohama
Yokohama, Japan

Left: Glass-enclosed Cafè Tosca symbolizes the hotel as garden.
Above: The ballroom attracts business meetings and weddings alike.
Below: Guestrooms are for luxurious comfort and relaxation.
Photography: Jaime Ardiles-Arce

Yokohama has welcomed foreign guests and ideas since the Meiji era, and its complex personality is mirrored in the recently completed Pan Pacific Hotel. Located on Yokohama Bay, the 484-room hotel is part of a new development in the Minato Mirai 21 district. The design by Hirsch Bedner Associates is a striking arrangement of Japanese and international decor that caters to two audiences. Businessmen appreciate the Pan Pacific as an elegant, contemporary hotel whose ballroom, meeting rooms and lounges offer high quality services. Yet shoppers in the mall at the nearby JR Sakuragicho Station enjoy its "different spaces" and three restaurants, while families seek out its exotic environment for weddings and other important events. The design concept interprets the interior as a serene residence set in a garden, applying rich materials, warm colors and luxurious textures to the architecture, furnishings, art, water and indoor plantings to create a memorable sense of place. Although the facility is Modern and expansive in volume and shape, it accommodates business and social activities with intimately scaled appointments in the best Japanese and international traditions. Like Yokohama, the Pan Pacific looks both East and West.

Above: The large atrium and hand-painted scarf greet arriving guests.
Right: The front desk is flanked by some of the hotel's many palm trees.

Hirsch Bedner Associates

Grand Hyatt Muscat
Muscat, Sultanate of Oman

Left: Public spaces are dramatic.
Below: One of six restaurants, with its own cuisine.
Bottom: Guestrooms offer cool comfort.
Opposite: The grand lobby is the hotel's heart.
Photography: Ken Kirkwood

Four- and five-star hotels in the Middle East zealously hew to the international style of interior design that is the standard for established global operators. However, there are always hoteliers who pursue their own dreams, and the five-star, 240-room Grand Hyatt Muscat, set in the thriving capital city of the Sultanate of Oman, recently redefined the image of luxury service and accommodations in its region. Hirsch Bedner Associates was commissioned to develop an interior design for the Grand Hyatt that would celebrate Arab heritage, and it employed architectural vernacular, Islamic patterns and indigenous materials inside a four-story, Kublah-style, horseshoe-shaped concrete structure to turn this vision into a sumptuous reality. The key to the design was a floor plan that placed an open-sided grand lobby—overlooking the ocean and mountains, anchored by floor-to-ceiling columns and topped by a luminous dome—at the crossroads of activity where all restaurants and function areas would cluster. Custom-designed transitional furnishings, including local artwork, furniture and accessories keyed to an earth- and jewel-toned palette, carried the cultural theme from public areas to guestrooms. So upscale guests, who typically stay from 7-10 days, can now sample world-class hospitality served in gracious, Arabic style.

Hirsch Bedner Associates

Mandarin Oriental Kuala Lumpur
Kuala Lumpur, Malaysia

Below: *A view of the lobby, showing gold leaf ceiling dome, inlaid marble floor and marble columns with carved wood capitals.*
Photography: *George Apostolides.*

Right: A typical guest-room.
Below right: Pacifica's Grill and Bar.
Bottom right: The Ballroom.

It would have been effortless for the developers of the new Mandarin Oriental Kuala Lumpur to follow a scheme that produced a successful Mandarin Oriental hotel in another Southeast Asian city not long before. Why argue with success? However, the Mandarin Oriental Kuala Lumpur hired Hirsch Bedner Associates to exceed local expectations by creating a breathtaking flagship hotel at City Centre in Malaysia's capital city that is now regarded as a showcase of Malaysian culture in its past, present and future forms. Considerable research was conducted by the designers on Malaysia's art, crafts and cultural history, along with current and projected trends in lodging, food service and entertainment. The goal was to enchant guests from the moment they reached for the large-scale entry doors, which were fitted with door handles custom carved in a traditional Kris design. To carry the spirit of tradition and modernity inside, many of the furnishings and building products were exclusively made for the .

room establishment based on traditional styles and custom designs. For all the pageantry, of course, the Mandarin Oriental Kuala Lumpur has emerged as a superior environment for lodging, dining, and business and social events. The graceful flow of space, the careful planning and design of the restaurants, ballroom, public spaces, guestrooms and other accommodations, and the abundance of timely building technologies and guest services remind guests that tradition and high technology both belong in today's Malaysia.

Above: *The Lounge on the Park is perfect for tea and relaxation.*
Right: *A typical guestroom bath is luxuriously appointed.*

Hnedak Bobo Group

104 South Front

Memphis

Tennessee 38103

901.525.2557

901.525.2570 (Fax)

www.hbginc.com

Hnedak Bobo Group

Grand Terrace Hotel & Bellissimo Spa
Tunica, Mississippi

Harrah's Joliet Hotel
Joliet, Illinois

Top: Grand Terrace fire-place lobby.
Above: Grand Terrace lobby with front desk
Right: Harrah's Joliet main lobby.
Photography: Jeffrey Jacobs (Grand Terrace), Bob Greenspan (Harrah's Joliet)

Most casino hotels cater to customers who crave nonstop excitement. How might guests respond to a "soft Southern" casino hotel that is gracious and deliberate? If the 600-room Grand Terrace Hotel & Bellissimo Spa in Tunica, Mississippi, designed by Hnedak Bobo Group, offers insight, they will be enchanted. The entrance feels like a plantation home, complete with stone fireplace, cherry floors, granite counters, coffered ceilings, wrought iron hardware and 18th-century, English-style furnishings, and the imagery extends everywhere to put guests at ease. A different approach can be seen in the 2,000-square foot lobby of Harrah's Joliet Hotel, where Hnedak Bobo Group unified an eclectic setting. A variety of patterns, textures and materials, highlighted by a palette of gold, pewter and copper, inspires compliments from customers, who enjoy what they see.

Right: *Grand Terrace suite bedroom.*
Below: *Grand Terrace presidential suite.*

Hnedak Bobo Group

Themed Restaurants
East Chicago, Indiana and
North Kansas City, Missouri

Right: French Quarter
banquette seating.
Below left: Hallway to
banquet seating.
Below right: Diamond
Club VIP Lounge bar.
Opposite above:
Range entry.
Opposite below: Range
exhibition grill.
Photography: Bob
Greenspan

Restaurants serve a cornucopia of styles and themes to offer customers more than food and beverage, and Hnedak Bobo Group's work for the French Quarter Steakhouse and Diamond Club VIP Lounge, at Harrah's East Chicago, and the Range Steakhouse, at Harrah's North Kansas City, shows how delectable they can be. Diners seeking quiet luxury appreciate the French Quarter's deep carpeting, curled chandeliers and mahogany-stained beams, stairwell, wine racks and booths. A contemporary feeling is yours in the curving ceiling and counters, diamond patterned wood doors and columns and art glass of the Diamond Club. As for a campfire gathering in the Wild West, the space encircling the grill in the Range's pine, leather, slate, wrought iron and faux rock setting could draw sighs from old cowhands.

Hnedak Bobo Group

Winning Streaks Stadium Cafe
East Chicago, Indiana

Gaming customers arrive at Harrah's East Chicago casino ready for action, expecting the 196-seat Winning Streaks Stadium Cafe to deliver. And deliver it does. Once patrons enter the café, they head to one of four dining rooms designed by Hnedak Bobo Group that draw on sports venues in nearby Chicago for inspiration. The environment aims directly at fans of baseball, football, basketball and hockey, with a bar decked in Indy gear at the heart of the café to please auto-racing enthusiasts. In the baseball zone, for example, custom murals, festive bunting, dugouts with benches and a locker dedicated to Cubs' slugger Sammy Sosa practically recreate Wrigley Field. Similar techniques work their magic in the football, basketball and hockey zones, giving customers a front row seat to excitement. Wherever customers choose to dine at the café, everyone emerges a winner.

Above: Façade facing Harrah's rotunda.
Below: Basketball zone.
Opposite: Bar with pole-position tower.
Photography: Bob Greenspan

The Grand Ole Opry has come a long way from its birthplace in Nashville, Tennessee's Ryman Auditorium. Now, the Opryland Hotel & Convention Center, a resort combining entertainment and meeting facilities, is extending its brand into new markets, as seen in Grapevine, Texas, Orlando, Florida and Prince George's County, Maryland. Though each new Opryland will reiterate what has become the resort's signature feature, the glass-covered, climate-controlled atrium that functions as a town square with restaurants, retail shops and other attractions, it will also turn to vernacular architecture and interior design for inspiration. Thus, the two

million-square foot, 1,500-room Opryland Hotel Texas will resemble an Old West establishment, the two million-square foot, 1,400-room Opryland Hotel Florida is modeled on contextual examples found within Key West, St. Augustine and the Everglades. In addition, the two million-square foot, 2,000-room Opryland Hotel Maryland features a Boardwalk. The resorts' blend of family entertainment and convention business will have others besides Country and Western music fans singing.

Above: *Opryland-Florida.*
Right: *Winery at Opryland-Texas.*
Below: *Boardwalk at Opryland-Maryland*
Illustrations: *Genesis Studios (Florida), Phil Hamilton (Texas), Howard & Assoc./Richard Reed (Maryland)*

Hornberger+Worstell

170 Maiden Lane
San Francisco, California 94108
415.391.1080
415.659.1812 (Fax)
design@hwiarchitects.com
www.hornbergerworstell.com

Hornberger+Worstell

Renaissance Esmeralda
Indian Wells, California

Golf is a serious avocation in Indian Wells. In fact, magnificent golf courses surround the Renaissance Esmeralda Resort on all sides. To fit the handsome, 590-room, 530,000-square foot Renaissance Esmeralda to its site, Hornberger + Worstell carefully aligned the hotel and its attendant outdoor spaces with the adjacent greens. Of course, golf was not the only reason for attracting guests to the resort. The building program called for superb conference facilities, including a grand ballroom, numerous meeting rooms, and extensive break out and function areas, all oriented towards a significant lobby acting as a visible focus for major events. This goal was successfully achieved by grouping mid-rise guestroom pavilions around a landscaped central lobby atrium, appointing the interiors with stone, copper and anaigre wood, and bathing the entire space in a palette of light, desert-compatible tones. On or off the links, doing business should be a pleasure at the Renaissance Esmeralda.

Above left: Break out lounge.
Top: Corridor off central lobby.
Above: Outdoor pool and grounds.
Opposite: Central lobby atrium.
Photography: Sally Painter Photography

162

Hornberger+Worstell

The W Hotel
San Francisco, California

A prime urban location in San Francisco's chic South of Market (SoMA) neighborhood next door to the San Francisco Museum of Modern Art (SFMoMA) and Yerba Buena Gardens, provided the backdrop for the latest W Hotel. Designed by Hornberger + Worstell as a freestanding, 428-room, 300,000-square foot, 30-story facility for hip, young customers, the pre-cast and granite structure is based on a public space podium supporting the guestroom tower. The

hotel fully exploits its compact site in creating effective accommodations for a restaurant, several bars, a ballroom and other meeting facilities, and back-of-house support services as well as guestrooms and suites with a bold, modern interior that also happens to be comfortable and warm. As could be expected, all guestrooms have Internet access through their TV sets, and such state-of-the-art building technologies as digital lighting controls.

Yet being steps from SFMoMA and its cultured neighbors, the W attends to the aesthetic dimensions of its guests' stay by immersing them in a striking environment crafted from such materials as polished granite, mahogany, hand set fine carpet and fabrics, and terrazzo. Life imitates art, at the W.

Left: *Entry lobby.*
Above: *Exterior elevations.*
Photography:
Whittaker Photography

Above left: Meeting rooms with windows.
Above: Guest bathroom.
Left: Lobby lounge.

Hornberger+Worstell

Westin La Cantera Resort
San Antonio, Texas

How do you place a 500-room, half-a-million-square foot hotel at the crest of a prominent limestone butte on the outskirts of San Antonio? Very gently. Hornberger + Worstell has envisioned the Westin La Cantera Hotel as a village-like cluster of buildings that seem firmly rooted to the Texas Hill Country. The wings and pavilions of varying heights address the complex functional relationships between public and service spaces, keeping much back of house depressed below the sloping grade, and preserving the ancient cedar forest that encircles the site and is woven into its court-yards. Guests are deliber-ately treated to a less technical and more fun-damental image when they approach the thick plaster walls, native limestone corner towers and red clay tile roofs that give the Westin La Cantera Resort and its nearby casitas of suites and executive pavilions their vernacular spirit.

Above: *Entrance to the bar.*
Left: *The Hotel on the crest of a butte.*
Opposite: *Living room in a casita.*
Photography: *Henry L. Fechtman.*

Inside, they see further evidence of traditional South Texas life through the textured plaster walls, articulated heavy timber beams, large profile stained moldings, massive Spanish cedar plank doors, wall paneling and shutters, and rustic bronze and wrought iron hardware, handrails and gates. This is as good as life gets in Old San Antonio.

Above: Careful architectural massing reduces the bulk of the Westin La Cantera Resort.
Right: The grounds are carefully integrated with the ancient cedar forest.

Howard Snoweiss
Design Group

A division of RTKL Associates Inc.

4200 Aurora Street

Coral Gables

Florida 33146

305.461.3131

305.461.3330 (Fax)

Howard Snoweiss Design Group

The Point of Aventura, Atlantic III
Aventura, Florida

Buoyed by trade between the United States and Latin America, the greater Miami real estate market is raising the standards for luxury residences. An outstanding example is the public space in a 31-story, 168-unit condominium, The Point of Aventura, Atlantic III, in Aventura, a northern suburb of Miami, designed by Howard Snoweiss Design Group.

Home buyers are pleased that the "warm, residential feeling" at The Point of Aventura translates into such amenities as a spa, wine cellar, garden room, library and card room, in addition to a two-story main lobby with mezzanine. This ambitious program has given the designers ample opportunity to develop dramatic floor plans that are realized through graceful archi-

tectural forms, fine furnishings and opulent materials. Highlights of the design include the two-story main lobby, spiral staircase, curved walls, ceiling domes and a spectacular water feature, which collectively make a visitor's arrival a dramatic and memorable event. It's an ideal setting for such finishes as Juperano gold granite, emperor green marble, Saturnia travertine, fig-

ured anigre, cherry, mahogany, contemporary-style fabrics and carpets, and beveled and etched glass—and an ideal place for successful people to call home.

Above: A view past the mezzanine and ceiling domes.
Opposite: A lounge lets guests pause at the concierge desk.
Photography: Roy Quesada Photography.

Left: The library serves readers and conversationalists.
Above: Water-jet cut stone floors add their figuration.

Howard Snoweiss
Design Group

The Pinnacle
Sunny Isles, Florida

Left: *The Art Deco-style interior recalls the Miami of the 1920s.*
Far left: *Rich upholstery fabrics make residents and guests feel at home.*
Opposite: *Spiral stairs and a radial soffit put a spin to the central lobby.*
Above: *A skylight-style ceiling make this one-story space feel spacious.*
Photography: *Thomas Delbeck Photography.*

Whether or not the 242-unit Pinnacle is truly "Miami's First and Only Five-Star Condominium," as its developer proclaims, the design of the public space by Howard Snoweiss Design Group has successfully transformed four remote elevator lobbies and their circuitous connecting hallways into a coherent, elegant and hospitable environment. The designers organized the elevator lobbies as formal and symmetrical "anchors" served by informal, curvilinear and bridge-like corridors. An updated, Art Deco-style signature look worthy of a world-class hotel and resort was created for the space by drawing on architectural elements and furnishings appropriate to South Florida, such as the French limestone floors, custom-woven Tibetan carpet, baby grand piano, anigre veneers, solid mahogany, bronze and brass hardware and trim, contemporary furniture, two-story-high water feature, radial soffits and spiral staircase in the central lobby. What about residents wanting hotel-style services? The facility would make room for a rich menu of amenities that included valet, concierge and security stations, combined meeting/party room, cigar lounge, kitchen and bar, card room, library, mail room, special accommodations for young children and teenagers, and a fully-staffed spa. Five-star hotel guests should be so fortunate.

Howard Snoweiss
Design Group

Ritz-Carlton Amelia Island
Amelia Island, Florida

Below: The heart of the café displays its informal, Florida plantation style.
Right: Bronze fish and custom lighting fixtures lend a distinctive character.
Photography: Nancy Robinson Watson.

Below: The dessert bar is enriched by a copper and glass tile mosaic.
Bottom left: An Old World flavor is introduced under the entrance's patina finished dome.

How does a luxury, oceanfront resort turn an existing, 5,200-square foot formal dining room into a lighter and more contemporary café? For the 449-room Ritz-Carlton on Florida's Amelia Island and the Howard Snoweiss Design Group, the solution is to take a casual approach. The recent renovation keeps less than half of the original perimeter, as banquette walls were pulled back and perimeter sites were cleared for a bar and two repositioned buffets. A new entrance hints at a Florida plantation-style setting with a floor of marble and travertine, walls of raffia paneling and an elliptical patina finished dome. The eloquently, articulated, casual theme is exuberantly developed in the café through such furnishings as wicker and rattan armchairs, custom iron chandeliers and sconces of Murano glass and faux alabaster, a bar with marble top and copper, brass and mirrored accents, a dessert bar backed by copper and glass mosaic tiles, custom Axminster carpet depicting underwater life, and whimsical accessories like bronze fish, glass sea turtles and paintings of indigenous birds. Who can resist this charming invitation to taste the delights of a legendary island 35 miles northeast of Jacksonville, endowed with a colorful, 19th-century historic district and 13 miles of stunning beaches?

Howard Snoweiss
Design Group

Royal Caribbean International
Voyager of the Seas

There is only one Royal Suite aboard the Voyager of the Seas, the world's largest cruise ship at 1,020 feet in length, with 1,546 rooms for 3,118 passengers, and an ice skating rink inaugurated by Olympian Katarina Witt. The well-appointed, 1,042-square foot suite, designed by Howard Snoweiss Design Group, epitomizes luxury with its spacious entry foyer, living and dining area with wet bar, bedroom suite with full bath and powder room, service pantry and balcony. Equally impressive is its use of such fine materials and furnishings as anigre and mahogany, marble and travertine, silk and mohair, and custom-designed furniture. Of course, the stately flow of space, elegant architecture and luxurious appointments conceal inspired solutions to the ship's structure and technical equipment. However, making challenges in naval architecture seem effortless is one reason why the work of Howard Snoweiss Design Group is often at sea.

Above left: The bedroom suite features a circular bed and numerous amenities.
Above right: A baby grand piano dramatizes the entry to the living area.
Left: Marble sets the mood for the luxurious bathroom and powder room.
Photography: Thomas Delbeck Photography.

IA

350 California Street
Suite 1500
San Francisco
California 94104
415.434.3305
415.434.0330 (Fax)
www.ia-global.com

Atlanta
Boston
Chicago
Costa Mesa
Dallas
Denver
Ft. Lauderdale
Hong Kong
London
Los Angeles
Miami
Minneapolis
New York
Philadelphia
Silicon Valley
Washington, DC

IA

Willie & Reed's
Bethesda, Maryland

Above: Lower dining room with bar, upper dining room and exposed ceiling.
Photography: Christian Molina

When is a sports bar not a sports bar? When it's Willie & Reed's in Bethesda, Maryland, designed by IA. Bethesda, a satellite office center and bed-room suburb of Washington, D.C., and headquarters of the National Institute of Health, is populated by well-educated, affluent and sophisticated people who already have numerous trendy restau-rants in their backyard. Consequently, the owners of 90-seat, 3,545-square foot Willie & Reed's decided to open a restaurant with a sports theme instead of just the latest sports bar. IA adopted the basic forms, finishes and visual ele-ments of a sports facility, including such details as open structure, stained

concrete floors, stainless steel panels and railings, and light-filtering banners, for its own design. Complications stemming from installing the first restaurant ever to occupy the space resulted in modifications to the base building for code compliance. Otherwise, IA focused on producing an environment with upper and lower dining rooms and a 20-seat bar that could draw the office crowd and residents alike.

A brisk lunch business and lines waiting to enter on weekend nights indicate a championship season for IA.

Above: *The view from the upper dining room.*
Right: *Banquette in booth configuration.*
Below right: *Bar counter and stools*

IA

Quilty's
Princeton, New Jersey

Left: Dining room under barrel vaulted ceiling.
Above: *Trains and ships show up in wall and banquette details.*
Photography: *Peter Cook*

Named for a worldly-wised playwright and roue in Vladimir Nabokov's unforgettable Lolita, Quilty's, in Princeton, New Jersey, was designed by IA to serve hearty, bistro fare in a 1930s-style setting that evokes memories of fast trains and sleek oceanliners. It's a sophisticated endeavor whose nuances are not lost on Princetonians, who reside in one of the most charming, affluent and well-educated communities—the site of the Princeton University campus—in the Northeast. The interior design combines rosewood wall panels, leather banquettes, mirrors, brass fixtures, custom lighting, marble counters, painted wall murals, ceramic tiles and carpet to create a 1,350-square foot space (excluding the kitchen) supporting two separate environments, a 10-seat bar and 60-seat dining room. Even if Quilty's has no way of straying from its physical moorings, it can transport customers to distant places of the mind that they can happily contemplate over a selection from the restaurant's well-informed wine list. Perhaps the restaurant could even be described, with an apology to "Papa" Hemingway, as a moveable feast.

Left: Wainscot and wall mural in bar area evoke 1930s...
Right: Semicircular booth holds banquette and mural.
Mural: Designed by Debra Regh.

Venture Frogs
San Francisco, California

Right: *Beaux Arts and high technology meet in the dining room.*
Photography: *Beatrice Coll*

Van Ness is a broad thoroughfare where many of San Francisco's most prominent citizens chose to build their elegant homes in the years before the earthquake of 1904. Today, the street thrives as a commercial environment populated by an eclectic and lively mix of shops, restaurants, movie theaters, offices, City Hall and such cultural treasures as the San Francisco Opera House and the Herbst Theater, and it regularly attracts an upscale and trendy crowd. Into this lively setting has come Venture Frogs, a 120-seat, 9,000-square foot restaurant in the historic lobby of 1000 Van Ness that combines the Beaux Arts charm of a 1920s building with the cerebral chic of high-tech materials and furnishings. The blending of aesthetic styles is not unlike the fare, which could be characterized as a fusion cuisine based on Asian noodles. The designers literally took the raw ingredients of Silicon Valley's products and facilities, such as mother boards, TV monitors, computer work stations, metal screens and fiber optics, and combined them into an interior design that manages to feel light-hearted and avant garde at the same time. Customers are drawn towards one of two well defined areas: the bar and the dining room. Each occupies its own distinct setting but remains discreetly visible to the other through metal beaded screens, which can be viewed from the various ban-

quette, booth and free-standing table settings. The bar, featuring a translucent, illuminated counter in which electronic components are imbedded, is the star of the space. But there's enough visual energy running through Venture Frogs so customers will feel themselves a part of this whimsical environment wherever they are seated.

Above: *Maitre d'hotel desk before row of booths.*
Left: *Bar top of imbedded high-tech gear with matching stools.*

Kenneth E. Hurd & Associates Inc.

21 Lexington Road

Lincoln

Massachusetts 01773

781.259.3300

781.259.1444 (Fax)

www.keha.com

Kenneth E. Hurd & Associates Inc.

The Waldorf=Astoria
New York, New York

Below: *The monumental Main Lobby displays the clock from the original Waldorf=Astoria.*
Opposite: *A vaulted ceiling and full-height windows set a stately rhythm for the Silver Corridor.*
Photography: *Edward Jacoby*

Heads of state who seldom agree on anything will put aside their differences—to stay at the legendary Waldorf=Astoria Hotel in midtown Manhattan. Such has been the allure of the 1,380-room Art Deco landmark, originally designed by Schultz & Weaver, that it has welcomed the rich, famous and powerful since opening day on October 1, 1931. Keeping the name, facility and legend bright for the past 19 years has been the responsibility of

Kenneth E. Hurd & Associates. Room by room and section by section, the architecture firm has carefully restored and dramatically enhanced such important spaces as the Park Avenue Lobby, the Main Lobby, the Grand Ballroom, and the Towers Lobby and Presidential Suite in the Waldorf Towers. Much of this effort, paradoxically, has involved reversing the effects of "modernization" in the 1950s and 1960s to replace tradi-

tional Beaux Arts ornamentation with the unadorned forms and surfaces of Modernism. Fortunately, Schultz & Weaver's work had been more often obscured than removed. For example, superb original details in the famed crossroads of VIPs, the Park Avenue Lobby, were promptly returned to their prominence, including 13 allegorical murals and an opulent "Wheel of Life" mosaic medallion created by French artist Louis Rigal.

Since the original millwork in the Main Lobby was not restorable, a horizontal frieze, derived from molds taken of the legendary elevator doors, was installed and cove lighted to lend a glamorous glow to the ceiling. Simultaneously, the heirloom clock from the original Waldorf=Astoria was retrofitted with a new and stylish housing to form the centerpiece of the Main Lobby floor.

Above: The Grand Ballroom in full Art Deco dress has been a staple of New York's social life.
Left: A view of the Neoclassical Art Deco elements show what supports the formal Jade Room.

However, the various projects have gone beyond textbook restoration to instill a new esprit. For instance, the two-tiered, 1,500-seat Grand Ballroom was restored to its former glory through the removal of numerous alterations, the revival of original Art Deco ornamentation, and the addition of such elements as a new lighting design, a 31,000-watt sound system, a carpet that complements the architecture, and a subtle, off-white and rose color scheme.

Below: Scale, form and brilliant color give character to the well-lighted Empire Room.
Right: The jewel-like Conrad Suite is characterized by understated opulence and detailing.

For the Presidential Suite in the Waldorf Towers, the luxurious suites on the top 14 floors of the hotel, the design firm conceived a rich, residential setting. Its 18th- and 19th-century-style furnishings typically surround presidents and kings in comfort, dignity and visual splendor. These and other special settings in the Waldorf=Astoria and the Waldorf Towers have served as proud milestones for Kenneth E. Hurd & Associates in its years of service to the hotel. After all, the hotel has occupied a central place in New York's social life for over a century.

Above: *The Towers Lobby receives VIP guests staying in the prestigious Waldorf Towers.*
Top: *The Presidential Suite bedroom combines splendid materials and intimate scale.*
Right: *A gracious residential-style living room forms the heart of the Presidential Suite.*

Right: The Cocktail Terrace and Cole Porter's piano give focus to the Park Avenue Lobby.
Below: Sir Harry's Bar combines sophistication and warmth in an urban milieu.

In another example of going beyond textbook restoration, the design firm transformed the raised portion of the Park Avenue Lobby from a storage area to a stunning terrace cocktail lounge overlooking Park Avenue, using a free-standing pavilion to feature Cole Porter's grand piano. Yet much remains, as it should. The first Waldorf= Astoria, founded as the Waldorf by William Waldorf Astor in 1893 and the Astoria by his cousin John Jacob Astor IV in 1897 on the future site of the Empire State Building, was one of the first places where New Yorkers could gather socially outside their homes. (It was to ward off any potential rivalry that the two names were separated by an equal sign.) The current Waldorf=Astoria, under the discerning eye of Kenneth E. Hurd & Associates, should satisfy this role with distinction for many generations of future New Yorkers.

Lieber Cooper Associates

444 North Michigan Avenue

Chicago

Illinois 60611

312.527.0800

312.527.3159 (Fax)

melissa@liebercooper.com

Lieber Cooper Associates

Nacional27
Chicago, Illinois

Right: View of ban-
quettes in arena dining
area.
Below: Semi-private
cocktail seating.
Photography: Mark
Ballogg/Steinkamp/
Ballogg Photography

You have to step lively to keep up with the crowd in Chicago's River North neighborhood, which is home to architects, antique dealers, advertising agencies, art galleries and a very cool Latin community. So Lieber Cooper Associates was happy to accept an assignment from Lettuce Entertain You Enterprises, one of the Windy City's top restaurateurs, to feed a growing interest in Nuevo-Latino cuisine and culture with Nacional27, a new restaurant occupying a River North space that the firm had previously designed for the same client. To provide a tantalizing hint of dining and dancing to passersby yet simultaneously preserve the guests' privacy, the designers superimposed one translucent screen over another starting with frosted glass at the storefront backed by sheer drapery, and to subdivide the theater-like space into private and semi-private dining areas grouped around a 20-foot diameter bamboo dance floor that is dramatically illuminated by soft pools of architectural lighting. Chicagoans who want to dance their way through the 27 nations of Latin America—the inspiration for "Nacional27"—now know where to begin their journey.

Below: Twenty-foot diameter dance floor in the main dining area.

Lieber Cooper Associates

Spiaggia
Chicago, Illinois

Left: *View towards bar.*
Opposite: *Main dining room.*
Photography: *Mark Ballogg/Steinkamp/ Ballogg Photography*

Sixteen days are a brief interval for most people, but a thriving restaurant would not close for more than two weeks unless it took an annual summer holiday. Nevertheless, Larry Levy of Levy Restaurants and chef Paul Bartollotta shared a vision to make the atmosphere of Chicago's Spiaggia equal its cuisine, and they enlisted Lieber Cooper Associates to make the changes with a construction shut-down window of only 16 days. Spiaggia's new design boasted a stunning minimal Modernist look. To save on cost and design, "center stages" were identified where building materials, art-work, lighting, decorative fabrics and colors would have the greatest impact. Large floor-to ceiling windows overlook Lake Shore Drive and the beach at the Magnificent Mile. The clerestory win-dows on the upper right allow views from Spiaggia's private dining rooms to the beach and main dining room. The floor plan reflected Renaissance order in its intimate areas, soaring main dining room, and such classic elements as arches and columns. Furnishings and acces-sories were decidedly Italian and contemporary with a touch of whimsy, right down to the live, sculptured topiaries. The Chicago Tribune's food critic Phil Vettel summed up the redesign as 'Simply stunning.'

Lieber Cooper Associates

Stackwoods
Lincoln, Nebraska

Right: Dining beneath open trusses.
Below: Ledgestone fireplace.
Photography: Mark Ballogg/Steinkamp/ Ballogg Photography

Right: Exterior and signage.
Below: Bar area.

If patrons of Stackwoods, a recently completed stand-alone, 320-seat restaurant in Lincoln, Nebraska feel they are coming home to a timeless American institution, it's only natural. Stackwoods represented an unusual opportunity for Lieber Cooper Associates, working with KK&E as architect, to create a total visual environment, from the logo that supports the food service concept to the architecture, interior design and graphics that present it. Beginning with the portrait of the Stackwoods Chef, a robust, congenial character depicted in a rectangular, wood cut-style logo, the visual branding of Stackwoods illustrated the idea of wood-fired American cooking as a traditional cornerstone of American life. The story of Stackwoods has been made visible in its exterior, a modern interpretation of the American barn vernacular, its expansive, vaulted interiors, and its handsome graphics, a coordinated ensemble of menus, packaging, mechandising materials, stationery, uniforms and

Upper left: *Logo design.*
Above: *Cashier and maitre d'hotel station.*
Lower left: *Built-in bookcases.*

signage. No detail was overlooked to make the visual experience satisfying for customers, including a massive, ledgestone fireplace, faux aged plaster finish, colorful ceramic tiles, sturdy wood floors, wainscot and furniture, and Midwestern landscape murals that recall artist Thomas Hart Benton. Before long, citizens of Lincoln craving hearty, wood-fired American fare in the perfect setting may need no prompting to head straight to Stackwoods.

Lynn Wilson Associates
International

116 Alhambra Circle

Coral Gables

Florida 33134

305.442.4041

305.443.4276 (Fax)

lwai@bellsouth.net

Lynn Wilson Associates International

Al Bustan, Dubai
United Arab Emirates

Below: The lush and spacious atrium lobby forms the heart of Al Bustan.
Bottom left: A famous London-Indonesian-Thai style restaurant named Blue Elephant.
Bottom: Appealing and sophisticated Benihana restaurant.
Photography: Courtesy of the Hotel Al Bustan.

Petroleum's impact on the United Arab Emirates can be assessed on the skyline of Dubai, where modern skyscrapers, shopping centers and hotels keep rising to serve the liveliest Gulf city. It's here that the new hotel Al Bustan welcomes guests to elegant, transitional contemporary interiors designed by Lynn Wilson Associates International. The design succeeds not only by creating an atrium lobby to unite all of the six-story, 400,000-square foot hotel's public spaces. It also provides winning interiors for the restaurants, prefunction rooms and guestrooms that combine sophisticated design with timeless comfort. Why shouldn't guests be able to conclude a day of camel racing or shopping in the gold souqs by returning to Al Bustan for relaxation and perhaps some Web surfing in their guestrooms before sampling Dubai's famed night life?

Above: *Royal penthouse suite for his Royal Highness Sheik Hamden Maktoum accommodations make long stays pleasurable.*
Right: *Arab themes are present in this Lebanese restaurant, complete with belly dancers.*

Lynn Wilson Associates International

Panama Marriott
Panama City, Panama

What place does a superb, new, five-star, 16-story, 230-room hotel have in Panama City? A very important place, if you're talking about the recently completed Panama Marriott, designed by Lynn Wilson Associates International. Sprawling on the Pacific coast just east of the Panama Canal, Panama City is a thriving center of banking and trade. Its cosmopolitan flair is visible in its diverse population of 700,000 and the infinite variety of its restaurants, night clubs and shops, and it exerts a strong influence on the hotel's lobby, lobby lounge, restaurant, sports bar, meeting/board room, ballroom, guestrooms, pool and terrace, business center and health club. While the Panama Marriott occupies a stringent floor area of 315,000 square feet, the designers have assembled the pieces and furnished and lighted them so skillfully that guests are likely to remember the grandeur and excitement rather than the dimensions—a treat they will want to taste again.

Below left: Champion's lounge is shaped by geometry and memorabilia.
Right: The lobby lounge invites guests to gather under its vaulted ceiling.
Below: This lobby bar is a reminder of Panama City's rich night life.
Photography: Courtesy of Panama Marriott.

Below: Elegant dining is
another facet of the
Panama Marriott.
Bottom left: Guestroom
appointments are on a
world-class level.
Bottom right: Business
people can count on fine
facilities like this.

Lynn Wilson Associates International

Marriott Los Sueños
Herradura Bay, Costa Rica

Anything can happen and often does in San Jose as the crowded, bustling capital of Costa Rica. One-and-half hours drive to the Pacific coast lies Costa Rica's premier destination resort, a former agricultural community that grew up overnight. However, beautiful traces of the pastoral life that once flourished, and persuasive evidence of a paradise can be seen at the new Marriott Los Sueños, designed by Lynn Wilson Associates International. The four-story, 400,000-square foot, 250-room hotel include a golf club, casino, shops, gallery along with a lobby, lobby lounge, two restaurants, conference area/ball-room, meeting room, pool and pool bar, and health club. The openness of the site resulted in the principal design challenge: How to create hotel facilities with an "inside/outside" atmosphere, because most

Left: The facades emphasize the open environment.
Above: A lounge displays the "inside/outside" atmosphere.
Top: Guests enjoy strolling down this vaulted colonnade.
Photography: Courtesy of Marriott Los Sueños

Top right: *A view of the sea favors many guestrooms.*
Right: *The outdoors never seems far from this lounge.*

functional areas—excluding the restaurants, conference facilities and guestrooms—would not have air conditioning. Consequently, much of Marriott Los Sueños will be experienced by guests as open-air, covered spaces with verandas joined by open circulation paths networked throughout the public and guest areas, all facing the sparkling blue Pacific Ocean with the world's most breathtaking sunsets.

Lynn Wilson Associates International

Pico Bonito Lodge
La Ceiba, Honduras

Left: The architecture and interior design are deliberately rustic.
Above: Beyond the Lodge is Pico Bonito national park.
Below: Guestrooms are housed in charming, one-story bungalows.
Photography: Courtesy of Pico Bonito Lodge.

As the third largest city in Honduras, La Ceiba is known for shipping bananas and pineapples marketed by Standard Fruit under the Dole name. But the days when Standard Fruit dominated La Ceiba are gone, and an appropriate symbol of the new order is the handsome Pico Bonito Lodge, designed by Lynn Wilson Associates International. Guests arrive at the rustic, 22,000-square foot facility to stay in one-story bungalows. Modern amenities are present, of course, along with a lobby, restaurants, lounge, pool and conference center, at the Lodge's jungle site with waterfalls and pools. Tourists bound for nearby Pico Bonito National Park love the Lodge, which opens a promising door to Honduras' future..

208

Morris ☆ Architects

800 N. Magnolia

Suite 1025

Orlando

Florida 32803   Orlando

407.839.0414   Houston

407.839.0410 (Fax)   Culver City

www.morrisarchitects.com   Mexico City

Morris ☆ Architects

Morris ☆ Architects

Portofino Bay Hotel
at UNIVERSAL Orlando a Loews Hotel
Orlando, Florida

Even as our heads tell us we are entering the dawn of the Internet era, our hearts keep taking us back to a pre-electronic frame of mind. That's why vacationers arriving at Universal Studios in Orlando can stroll through the romantic heart of what appears to be an Italian seaside village recreated at the Portofino Bay Hotel, a 750-room, 780,000- square foot Loews Hotel. A series of rivers and canals connect Portofino Bay with other hotels and attractions at UNIVERSAL Orlando, enabling Portofino Bay to evoke a rich illusion of life on the Mediterranean for guests enjoying the suites and guestrooms, two ballrooms, nine function/meeting rooms, a 10,600-square foot health spa, three swim-

Above: The approach to the Porte Cochere. **Left:** View of harbor side from the pier. **Photography:** UNIVERSAL Orlando; Eric Morgan, Morris Architects; Kevin Flanky

Right: *Piazza Centralle adjacent to the meeting rooms and lobby.*
Below: *Retail arcade.*
Below right: *Grand staircase from the registration area leading to the lower-level ballrooms.*

ming pools, one bocci ball court and a full-service business center. Because details count here, the design makes careful use of such elements as faux finishes, porcelain tile, authentic and reproduction fixtures, fine rugs, ceramic roof tile, transitional furniture with hand-painted ornamentation, and tromp l'oeil painting, all concealing the latest in "smart room" technology. This may be the shortest route to Italy in America.

Morris ☆ Architects

Emeril's® Restaurant Orlando Universal Studios City Walk® Orlando, Florida

Gourmets may claim that the proper way to experience New Orleans' crawfish pie, gumbo ya-ya or grilled Creole mustard-marinated quail with field peas and Andouille is to dine in the French Quarter, and they may be right. However, Emeril Lagasse, James Beard Award-winning chef and popular TV host of "The Essense of Emeril," and "Emeril Live" could seduce them with his new 255-seat, 11,700-square foot Emeril's at Universal Studios City Walk® in Orlando. Joining the ranks of three successful New Orleans establishments and two outposts in Las Vegas, one of the newest ventures was designed by Morris Architects to portray a cool, hip and decidedly "new" New Orleans. Working closely with Emeril and his staff, the designers placed a main dining room, private dining area, cigar room, wine rooms, bar, kitchen, wine storage and exhibition kitchen into an existing space. Customers attracted by the striking bar on the lower level that conveys them to the main dining room on the lower level are surrounded by an imaginative environment of industrial and natural materials. Who knows? Such details as precast stone walls, oak and maple floors and millwork, exposed ducts and tall wine cases reached by library ladders—plus Emeril's cuisine—may even lure gourmets to Orlando.

Above right: View of main dining room towards grand stair and cork wall.
Below right: Corridor with wine cases.
Opposite: Bar on lower level from southeast corner.
Photography: Raymond Martinot

212

Morris ☆ Architects

Moody Gardens Hotel
Galveston, Texas

Planted like a lush garden of paradise on storied Galveston Island is the 242-acre Moody Gardens complex. This "eco-tourist" resort attracts business travelers and families to the Moody Gardens Convention Center, Rainforest Pyramid, Discovery Museum, IMAX theaters and the largest aquarium in the Southwest. The idea that a tropical island hideaway would flourish here provided momentum for the Moody Gardens Hotel, a 300-room, nine-story facility designed by Morris Architects to cater to conventioneers and families as well as provide hands-on training for students in the hospitality industry. Determined to sustain the spirit of the Gardens, the designers created a hotel environment that offers such features as guestrooms with breathtaking views of Galveston, a dramatic, 750-square foot water attraction in the lobby featuring man-made boulders and cascading pools, a rooftop restaurant with vistas of the Gulf of Mexico. Plus, Offats Bayou features a 15,000-square foot ballroom, flexible meeting rooms, elegant and casual dining, spa and fitness facilities, indoor and outdoor pools, and a variety of other services. Like Moody Gardens, the hotel will surely be something guests write home about.

Above: *Exterior elevation.*
Below: *Outdoor pools with Gulf of Mexico in background.*
Photography: *Douglas Childs, Rick Muniz (exterior)*

Morris ☆ Architects

Kemah Boardwalk Inn
Kemah, Texas

America's boardwalks were a turn-of-the-century urban development that gave families in the central cities a chance to flirt with the sea and its diversions, and surviving examples remind us how colorful and appealing they could be. So to transform "Restaurant Row" in Kemah, a Houston suburb, into a 14-acre, family-oriented entertainment complex, Morris Architects looked to the early 20th century for inspiration. The successful outcome is complete with a carousel, 60-foot ferris wheel, tower slide, miniature train ride, dancing water fountains, multi-level shopping, restaurants and the Boardwalk Inn. The Inn, designed by Morris Architects is a casual, 56-room boutique hotel in the Gulf Coast vernacular. While the Boardwalk Inn primarily entertains leisure guests, it accommodates a 100-seat executive ballroom as well as over 25,000 square feet of retail stores on the first floor.

Shaded balconies that catch the breeze, a marble-and-wood lobby with a wrought-iron staircase, guestrooms furnished with oversized desks, chairs and ottomans, and period-style signage and ornamentation are some of the details that enhance the look. As Tilman Fertitta, chief executive of the developer, Landry's Seafood Restaurants, commented, "The Boardwalk is now part of what you do when you come to Houston, Texas." Saltwater taffy, anyone?

Above: Main entrance to the Kemah Boardwalk complex. *Below:* Waterfront Boutique Boardwalk Inn. *Photography:* Douglas Childs, Rick Muniz

Morris ☆ Architects

Fairfield Washington, DC
Old Town Alexandria, Virginia

Set in a picturesque neighborhood known for its cafes and boutiques, the new 88-room, seven-story Fairfield Washington D.C. at Old Town Alexandria, Virginia is the perfect solution for those seeking the best in urban living and old world charm. The timeshare's location, just a short, 10-minute drive across the Potomac River from the nation's capitol, and a two-minute walk to the metro system, is incomparable. Morris Architects' design concept for the timeshare resort evolved as a residential urban solution that began with an extensive survey to determine the design elements that would best complement the graceful surrounding structures of historic Old Town Alexandria. The building's classical Georgian detailing, interpreted through the red brick exterior with cast stone trim, is a graceful solution, while the dramatic, full-height atrium and the building's integration with the adjacent structures serve to counteract the constraints of the tight urban site.

In addition to on-premises amenities such as a central atrium garden, hospitality/breakfast area, a fitness center, arcade and retail shops, the resort's location as one of three buildings within the King Street Metroplace complex affords residents easy access to additional amenities in the adjacent Hilton Hotel and office building.

Above: *Atrium Garden.*
Below: *A garden terrace and outdoor dining area face the entry main entry/motor court from King Street, renowned as the historic street in all of Old Town Alexandria.*
Photography: *Alan Karchmer.*

Morris Nathanson Design

1163 Exchange Street

Pawtucket

Rode Island 02860

401.723.3800

401.723.3813 (Fax)

www.morrisnathanson.com

Morris Nathanson Design

Burton & Doyle
Great Neck, New York

Left: A view of the façade displays its monumental forms.
Below left: The island bar generates energy for the entire facility.
Opposite: A mural, fine millwork and custom lighting blend perfectly.
Photography: Warren Jagger Photography, Inc.

When F. Scott Fitzgerald wrote The Great Gatsby in 1925, he placed his Flapper Era characters in the very real world of Long Island's Gold Coast, the cluster of exclusive North Shore communities where 'new money' vies for admission to the elite social circles dominated by 'old money' clans. Jay Gatsby and Friends would have loved Burton & Doyle, a new, 225-seat steakhouse in Great Neck, N.Y., designed by Morris Nathanson Design. The space evokes the splendid Gold Coast mansions built by such established families as the Roosevelts, Vanderbilts and Whitneys, and does so with an interior design that appears to speak directly to the young, affluent couples and "ladies who lunch," who praise its comfort and security. Thorough planning and comprehensive design have contributed significantly to the success of the steakhouse, which competes with similar establishments along Northern Boulevard, one of the area's busiest thoroughfares. Circulation flows gracefully from a monumental island bar that is perfect for conversation to a multi-level dining area where guests manage to be seen without surrendering their privacy. To complete the effect, the designers have gone to great lengths to get the details right, including superb architectural millwork, elegant custom lighting fixtures, a sweeping mural depicting the life of the "horsey set," a handsome cigar room and an elegant wine room. (Fine wine is displayed throughout the restaurant as a secondary theme.) Mr. Gatsby, your table is ready.

Morris Nathanson Design

Angelo & Maxie's Steakhouse
New York, New York

Above: The storefront has an early 20th century, New York look.
Left: Open kitchen activities add to the congeniality.
Below left: The bar is an informal source of entertainment.
Opposite: Pendant lighting, lettered frieze and mahogany paneling set the tone.
Photography: Warren Jagger Photography, Inc.

Like a thundering herd at roundup, Americans have returned to beef eating with gusto. A good place to watch the action is on New York's West 52nd Street, where Angelo & Maxie's, a steakhouse designed by Morris Nathanson Design, has opened at the headquarters of securities giant Paine Webber. The 275-seat, two-level restaurant targets young business executives seeking a popular, informal and affordable way to enjoy steak in the Big Apple. Accordingly, the physical environment is lighter, younger and more entertaining than most steakhouses. Guests enter by walking directly into the lively bar area before proceeding to the dining room, where they can view the bar at one end and the open kitchen at the other. The congeniality at the bar is reflected in such details as custom pendant light fixtures, a lettered frieze encircling the diners, and lightly stained mahogany paneling. Young men and women like the design so much that, Chart House, the new owner, will now use it for a nationwide rollout. That thundering herd may be coming to a neighborhood near you.

Morris Nathanson Design

Rue 57
New York, New York

You run into one interesting attraction after another by strolling along 57th Street in midtown Manhattan, including the flagship store of famed jeweler Tiffany & Company, the splendidly restored Carnegie Hall, an acoustic masterpiece named for industrialist Andrew Carnegie, the Art Students League, a venerable art school and hangout for generations of artists, and the bustling broadcast center for CBS News. One of the newest reasons to explore the street is a chance to visit Paris, if only for a meal, at Rue 57, a 140-seat, two-story restaurant designed by Morris Nathanson Design. Inspired by the all-night oasis of Parisian boulevardiers, such as, La Coupole, Rue 57 is an unabashed tribute to the French brasserie without being an actual replica. There is the same love of festive crowds, for example, which Rue 57 accommodates with wide, open spaces. Both have sturdy, comfortable seating, such as Rue 57's cozy banquettes and chairs. Warm pools of light stream from Rue 57's custom lighting fixtures

Top: *A sidewalk view of Rue 57.*
Above: *The seating mixes banquettes and separate tables.*
Opposite: *Rue 57's bar adds visual and acoustic life.*
Photography: *Warren Jagger Photography, Inc.*

and mirrors. Lively acoustics, a staple of La Coupole, are created in New York with ceramic tile floors. The restaurant happily engages the New York scene all the same, offering an American dream about a French restaurant that begins with a café-style storefront. When its French doors swing open, it attracts a diverse, upscale clientele that includes tourists, young people and guests from nearby hotels. Do they find the City of Light inside? Mais oui!

Right: *Downstairs has been designed to attract private parties.*
Below: *Finishes in burled wood and claret create a classic French color palette.*

Pamela Temples
Interiors, Inc.

7652 Ashley Park Court

Suite 306

Orlando, Florida 32835

407.298.9484

407.298.9184 (Fax)

www.pamelatemples.com

Pamela Temples Interiors, Inc.

Amelia Inn & Beach Club
Fernandina Beach, Florida

Left: The restaurant supports formal and casual dining.
Below: An elegant place setting for four.
Photography: Starling Productions, Inc., Orlando, Florida

Who would expect to find a relaxed crowd of vacationers and business people mingling casually in swimsuits, business attire and formal evening wear? It's an everyday phenomenon at the Amelia Inn & Beach Club, a resort flourishing at Fernandina Beach on Florida's Amelia Island. Making the cozy scene a reality was a major objective for Pamela Temples Interiors, Inc. in designing the 135,000-square feet of interiors for the four-diamond, 249-room hotel, conference center and beach club that were recently added to the original structure built in the 1970's. Other objectives included giving each guestroom an ocean view, creating highly functional ADA-compliant spaces, devising an easily navigable circulation plan, and designing aesthetically appealing settings for casual and formal events. The award-winning interior design, which received a Gold Award from the American Resort Development Association, incorporated natural elements

Above: The lobby/bar attracts many guests.
Right: A fireplace in the lobby/bar.

Pamela Temples Interiors, Inc.

Hilton Grand Vacations Club at the Las Vegas Hilton
Las Vegas, Nevada

Nobody makes odds on subtlety in Las Vegas, so visitors to the Hilton Grand Vacations Club at the Las Vegas Hilton cannot help noticing its intriguing, relaxing and calming qualities. In fact, these are the qualities that guided Pamela Temples Interiors, Inc. in designing a facility to sell dwelling units at the Hilton Grand Vacations Resort, not far from the 30-story Las Vegas Hilton Hotel. The Sales Center establishes a sequence of events from the Entry/Lobby area to the Discovery area, the Presentation Galleries and the Closing area, and frames an array of audio/visual technologies in reassuring, contemporary custom cabinetry and off-the-shelf furnishings. Drawing on the desert skyline rather than the casinos for inspiration, the interior designers also developed a Vacation Ownership Unit featuring stylish, custom-designed yet durable fabrics and case goods in a soothing, monochromatic, desert-inspired color palette to welcome buyers after a day of gaming, entertainment and shopping. Subtlety never scored so high before in Las Vegas.

Above: Sales Center's Entry/Lobby.
Right: Cabinetry detail in Owners Lounge.
Photography: Starling Productions, Inc., Orlando, Florida

Above: Living room for socializing and media.
Right: Guestroom with sitting area.
Far right: Master bedroom with jacuzzi tub in soothing desert palette.

Pamela Temples Interiors, Inc.

The Registry Resort
Naples, Florida

Right: Custom artwork in Café Chablis coordinates with fabrics and menu covers.
Below: Café Chablis.
Photography: Starling Productions, Inc., Orlando, Florida

Left: Deluxe Suite bedroom.
Right: Deluxe Suite living room.
Below right: Deluxe Suite dining room.

Midwesterners wondering where their "snowbirds" go in winter can often find them in Naples, Florida, where they may be enjoying the Café Chablis or the Deluxe Suite at the Registry Resort, both newly remodeled by Pamela Temples Interiors, Inc. Management and guests have marveled over the impact of inexpensive changes, such as faux finishes, upholstery fabrics that are repeated in the artwork and menus, reconfigured wood lattice panels, lush indoor plants and a new, private dining area, on the 10,000-square foot Café. For the Deluxe Suite, the challenge was to reflect the "quiet side" of the hotel, and the designers responded with a scheme that featured a palette of tone on tone in gold hues with black accents, furnishings that adhered to the grace and ease of the existing space, and dazzling materials and treatments that could withstand daily wear and tear. The resulting environment has had a wondrously serene if opulent effect on guests that should lure many a "snowbird" back for the winter.

Pamela Temples Interiors, Inc.

Hyatt Regency Pier Sixty-Six
Ft. Lauderdale, Florida

Left: African style living room.
Above: Admiralty suite dining room.
Below: A living room view of Ft. Lauderdale.
Photography: Starling Productions, Inc., Orlando, Florida

Hotel guests in Ft. Lauderdale can escape the busy metropolis just by entering one of six deluxe suites at the Hyatt Regency Pier Sixty-Six. To provide memorable lodging for VIP guests, Pamela Temples Interiors, Inc. reconfigured the suites for maximum efficiency, used existing and new furniture, and introduced distinctive themes. The Admiralty Suite, for example, evokes the Antilles Islands through tropical fabrics, exotic case goods and bright colors. By contrast, the Mercedes Suite recalls a 1940's vision of the English in Africa through furniture of teak, rattan and leather, leopard prints and dark woods. It's make-believe that's very real to VIP guests.

Paul Steelman Design Group

3330 West Desert Inn Road

Las Vegas

Nevada 89102

702.873.0221

702.367.3565 (Fax)

www.paulsteelman.com   Toronto, Canada

info@paulsteelman.com   Byranston, South Africa

Paul Steelman Design Group

The Regent Las Vegas at Summerlin
Summerlin, Nevada

Twenty-five minutes northwest of the Las Vegas Strip is affluent Summerlin, where fine homes, golf courses and spectacular views of the Las Vegas Valley make the gaming world seem lightyears away. For this reason, Paul Steelman Design Group has designed The Regent Las Vegas at Summerlin, a 54-acre, $270-million project, to emphasize luxury living rather than gaming. In fact, The Resort's nine buildings, including the six-story, 300-room hotels, The Regent Grand Palms and The Regent Grand Spa, go to great lengths to blend with the desert landscape. Even though the casino at The Regent welcomes guests with two high-limit areas, 1,200 slot machines and 40 table games for craps, black-jack, roulette, baccarat and the like, the hotel focuses on its connection to the 40,000-square foot, European-style Aquae Sulis Spa with such complementary facilities as a salon, boutique, workout area, aerobics studio, and 36 treatment areas for massages and other specialties. Richly detailed, transitional-style interiors drawing on the American West vernacular pamper guests in a subtle, luxurious and satisfying milieu where the casino is just part of the action.

Top: Exterior elevations.
Right: Grand Spa's main lobby.

Right: Cigar bar and lounge.
Below: Restaurant entry terrace.

235

Paul Steelman Design Group

Spiedini Restaurant
Las Vegas, Nevada

Above: Entrance.
Left: Main dining room.

Las Vegas likes environments to engulf guests in a world of rich forms, colors and textures where time and space are suspended. For this reason, the recent launch of Spiedini at The Regent Las Vegas was a bold move by architect Paul Steelman and his partner, master chef Gustav Mauler. The model for the 140-seat restaurant was the contemporary look of Milan, Italy's design and fashion center, and the partners gambled that Las Vegas would savor the difference. Combining such design elements as custom, circular pendant lighting, cove-lighted, circular soffits, finely tailored, circular banquettes, an 8-seat bar with floor-to-ceiling wine cellar and library ladder, and surfaces of brushed aluminum, hardwood and stone, they displayed the cool elegance of contemporary design free of historical allusions. Did they beat the odds? Waiting lists have guests lining up for lobster-filled ravioli, gnocchi in vodka cream sauce, orange in orange caramel sauce and a tasteful interior that Las Vegas obviously relishes.

Paul Steelman Design Group

Treasure Island
Las Vegas, Nevada

Below: *The lobby*

You don't have to imagine yourself as Captain Kidd, Sir Francis Drake or any other historic or fictitious pirate who ravaged the high seas to have a wonderful time at Treasure Island, a development of The Mirage in Las Vegas. This themed salute to the golden age of sailing ships is a 2,900-room hotel featuring such amenities as Buccaneer Bay, where the crews of H.M.S. Britannia and Hispaniola battle with cannon and musket every 90 minutes in the evening, Mutiny Bay, an amusement center offering interactive video, virtual reality, midway and arcade games, a pool, a salon and spa, 18,000-square feet of convention space, two wedding chapels, a variety of shops and four fine dining restaurants. Yet even strong themes can welcome variations. Paul Steelman Design Group has recently redesigned the lobby to season the rich experience awaiting guests with more subtle references to the pirate theme, and the happy result is enchanting sailors and landlubbers alike.

Paul Steelman Design Group

Desert Inn Resort and Casino
Las Vegas, Nevada

Right: *Façade and pool.*
Below: *Renaissance style suite.*
Opposite: *Entrance lobby.*

Understatement may attract attention when everything else is going over the top. The 715-room Desert Inn in Las Vegas, fondly known by its initials as the "DI," has eschewed the widespread obsession with thematic design in a recent renovation by Paul Steelman Design Group that creates its own magic. The Desert Inn is not austere, however. Working with the historic vocabularies so brilliantly orchestrated in the 1920's by architect Addison Mizner on Florida's gilded East Coast, the designers have bestowed a lively new spirit on the hotel's five structures. Guests take notice the moment they arrive in the grand entrance lobby, which honors Mizner's Palm Beach with a lobby atrium that soars seven stories above a polished marble floor and carved granite fountain, clad in Mizner's hallmark Spanish, Moorish and Mediterranean motifs. This expansive and luxu-

Right: Suite living room.
Below left: Suite dining room.
Below right: Evening view.

rious spirit is conveyed throughout the interiors. Guestrooms, which range in size from 400-square foot standard double rooms to penthouse suites of 1,530-4,000 square feet, all draw from the same rich sources that produced the duplex and multi-room high-roller suites of up to 9,300 square feet. As for the 20,000-square foot spa, the designers have interpreted the concept of elegance in a global range of historical and cultural contexts that should give guests a seemingly endless source of wonder. That the Desert Inn also boasts the one golf course on the Las Vegas Strip only adds to the luster of an establishment whose initials say everything.

RTKL

Baltimore	**Memphis**
410.528.8600	901.624.1600
Dallas	**London**
214.871.8877	44 (0) 20.7306.0404
Washington	**Tokyo**
202.833.4400	81 (0) 3.3583.3401
Los Angeles	**Hong Kong**
213.627.7373	852.2166.8944
Chicago	**Madrid**
312.704.9900	34 (0) 91.426.0980
Denver	
303.790.4130	www.rtkl.com

RTKL

St. Andrews Old Course Hotel
St. Andrews, Scotland

Below left: *Old meets new at the entry lobby.*
Below right: *The Hotel and the Old Course.*
Photography: *Scott McDonald, Hedrich-Blessing*

Imagine the surprise golfers felt in arriving at Scotland's legendary St. Andrews Old Course, the birthplace of the game five centuries ago, only to check into a 25-year-old hotel that scarcely acknowledged its surroundings, and you know what inspired the architecture firm of RTKL to renovate and expand St. Andrews Old Course Hotel with the interior design firm of Wilson & Associates. As planner, architect, graphic designer and coordinator of the design team, RTKL created a visual setting befitting the site—next to the 17th hole—and the sport. The exterior saw the addition of a pitched slate roof, the replacement of existing balconies with traditional wrought-iron ones, the addition of French doors, traditional glazing and cast-stone cornices, and the resurfacing of concrete walls in stucco-like harl. Inside, RTKL relocated ground-floor circulation corridors to face the golf course, consolidated three floors of accommodations into 125 deluxe guestrooms, enlarged and remodeled the 8,000-square foot spa, renovated the pro shop, and introduced a new lap pool under a glass-domed pavilion and a new, 30,000-square foot ballroom/meeting room. After five centuries, St. Andrews finally has a hotel fitting the spactacular envoronment surrounding it.

Right: *A new lap pool under glass.*
Opposite: *The interiors enjoy glorious views of the Old Course.*

RTKL

Amstel Inter•Continental
Amsterdam, The Netherlands

Right: *The pool in the new addition.*
Opposite: *A resplendent Grand Hall.*
Photography: *Scott McDonald, Hedrich-Blessing*

The architectural world's dowagers may look magnificent to the casual eye, but they often stand on trembling structural legs. Such was the case when RTKL assumed responsibility for renovating and expanding the great Amstel Inter-Continental, a hotel that has reigned on the Amstel River in the heart of Amsterdam since 1866. Restoring the seven-story, brick, stone and timber building was complicated by its crumbling foundation, the result of weak, old pilings, and an anticipated steel structure that was found to be unsupported brick, which required new steel columns. Foundation work was not the only challenge for RTKL and associate architect Erik Lopes Cardozo, of course. The façade and historically listed interior spaces such as the ballroom and Grand Hall were meticulously restored and discreetly given state-of-

the-art building systems, 111 tired guestrooms were transformed into 79 luxury guestrooms, and a 1960s extension was demolished and replaced by a brick-and-cast-stone addition housing a 97-seat restaurant, a leisure center with swimming pool, health club and spa, and a classically designed conservatory for the lobby lounge. How does this dowager feel today? Lively enough to win its five-star rating .

Above: *The lobby lounge in a conservatory.*
Right: *A view from the Amstel River.*

RTKL

Club Industrial de Monterrey
Monterrey, N.L., Mexico

Above right: *Façade and mountains.*
Right: *A dining room with a view.*
Below right: *An intimate lounge area.*
Opposite: *Stairway at the entry level.*
Photography: *Scott McDonald, Hedrich-Blessing*

The mountainous locale of Monterrey, N.L., Mexico, almost demands ambitious architecture, and RTKL has responded with the design of the Club Industrial de Monterrey. Not only has the architect shaped the award-winning structure into a dynamic, five-level, 60,000-square foot form that abstractly echoes the terrain, it has furnished the interiors with panoramic views of the mountains and the cities of Monterrey and Garza Garcia. Spaces flow gracefully into one another, starting with a 350-space parking garage at the plinth base and rising to include an events hall on the lower level, formal dining on the entry level, private dining rooms on the two upper levels, and administrative space on the mezzanine. Equipped with advanced building systems that can handle future expansion, the Club gives its members an exciting aerie to survey their world.

RTKL

Wyndham Hotel at Playhouse Square Cleveland, Ohio

Left: The Wyndham's triangular exterior.
Right: Stairway from ballroom to lobby.
Below: The registration desk.
Below right: A view of the restaurant.
Photography: Scott McDonald, Hedrich-Blessing

Cleveland's Playhouse Square District boasts four theaters listed on the National Register of Historic Places. Naturally, when Wyndham Hotels developed a triangular site at the entry to the District, it asked RTKL to design the new Wyndham Hotel to serve as a welcoming symbol. The 205-room facility that resulted features a lobby, restaurant and bar and guest registration area on the first floor, grand ballroom and meeting rooms on the second and third floors, and health club below grade, all keyed to active guests who are savvy enough to sample the city's great music and art as well as its drama during their stay.

Sandy & Babcock
International

1349 Larkin Street

San Francisco

California 94109

415.673.8990

415.441.3767 (Fax)

sbint@sandybabcock.com

www.sandybabcock.com

Sandy & Babcock International

Anassa Hotel & Spa
Polis, Cyprus

Cascading down a small rise on the Akamas Peninsula of Cyprus to a private beach and the Mediterranean Sea is what appears to be a charming Greek-Cypriot village with cosmopolitan residents. This vision is in fact the 184-room, 150,000-square foot Anassa Hotel & Spa, designed by Sandy & Babcock International with Cyprus-based Alecos Gabrielides Architect as local architect and James Northcutt Associates and Darrell Schmitt Design Associates as interior designer. Since the luxury hotel occupies Cyprus' relatively undeveloped northwestern coast, it functions as a self-contained community offering numerous guest activities. Its whitewashed walls and low-pitched tile roofs celebrate the vernacular in the form of a main hotel with a magnificent rotunda surrounded by a church, shops, restau-

rants, a taverna and guest villas. Also on display are such local touches as blue shutters, wrought iron railings, marble and hand-laid tile mosaic floors, furniture of wrought iron, wicker and rattan, wood and upholstery, exquisite rugs and textiles, and ancient pottery and artwork selected by the owner. With four restaurants, 7,000-square foot spa, outdoor and indoor pools, tennis courts on 65 acres, the Anassa may indeed have everything its guests could wish.

Above: A guestroom open to the sea.
Right: The view from the main hotel.
Photography: Henri Del Olmo

250

Above: The main hotel and guest villas.
Right: Entering the main hotel's rotunda.
Far right: An example of Greek-Cypriot vernacular.

Sandy & Babcock International

Fisher Island
Miami, Florida

Above: Above
Biscayne Bay.
Top: Island-style
hospitality.
Right: Homage to
Addison Mizner.
Opposite above:
Indoor/outdoor setting.
Opposite below:
Island Marina.
Photography: Steven
Brooke, Paul Barton

You must take a private ferry from the mainland to reach Fisher Island, set in Biscayne Bay just off the coast of Miami Beach. That suited William K. Vanderbilt, II when he built his Mediterranean-style estate on the 216-acre island in the 1920s, and that's how residents and guests like the exclusive resort and residential community today. Sandy & Babcock International has served as Fisher Island's sole planner and architect throughout its 18-year development and several different owners, creating and sustaining the illusion of a Mediterranean hill town on the flat island as it progresses towards the build-out of some 860 luxury second homes. But there is more to a community than housing, so the architects have presided over the addition of such facilities as The Inn at Fisher Island, a Spa Internazionale, a championship, Pete Dye-designed, 9-hole golf course with a 5,000-square foot clubhouse, a 16-court tennis club, a marina and a 32,500-square foot commercial center with shops, restaurants and other services. Their award-winning architecture draws on Vanderbilt's estate and Florida's heritage, particularly the work of Addison Mizner, to sustain one of the world's most exclusive residential addresses.

Sandy & Babcock International

Dharmawangsa Hotel & Spa
Jakarta, Indonesia

Since Kebayoran Baru emerged in the early 1940s as a "garden city" to become one of Jakarta's finest residential neighborhoods, the addition of the 100-room Dharmawangsa Hotel to a mixed-use development covering an entire city block called for an environment of intimacy and splendor. Sandy & Babcock International's acclaimed design provides both: a quiet retreat for executives with guestrooms 550-2,200 square feet in size, two restaurants, a ballroom, and numerous smaller meeting facilities, linked to Club Bimasena, a new, 50,000-square meter, world-class spa, fitness and dining club also designed by the firm. The hotel's bulk is downplayed as a series of separate, terraced sections, rising from a single-story entry pavilion with a four- and five-story front section to a nine- to ten-story rear section. Aside from incorporating such classic Indonesian architectural elements as shallow roof pitches, deep overhangs, clay tile roofs, massive columns, and gardens on three-fourths of the site, the hotel features such amenities as two elevator cores, soaring ground floor spaces, and interiors that reflect Indonesia's various cultural traditions. It's a bird's eye view of Indonesia for guests at the top of the business world.

Below: *The gracious, understated exterior.*
Photography: *Tim Street-Porter*

Above: Principal corridor to the entry pavilion.
Top right: Typical guestroom.
Above right: Outdoor dining.
Right:
Bath appointments.

Sandy & Babcock International

The Country Club
at The Diplomat
Hallandale Beach, Florida

To encourage guests of the 1,000-room Diplomat Hotel at Hallandale Beach, Florida to enjoy an enticing menu of activities, Sandy & Babcock International recently designed the handsome, 111,400-square foot Diplomat Country Club. The facility encompasses a 50,000-square foot golf club that complements a 6,700-yard course designed by Joe Lee with men's and women's lockers and lounge areas, a formal restaurant and an informal grille, bar and lounge, an 8,000-square foot conference center, a 30,000-square foot health and fitness spa, a 2,500-square foot, 10-court tennis club and 60 guestrooms and suites. All are housed in separate structures modeled in the style of a northern Italian villa and connected by covered breezeways. The Country Club has enhanced the appeal of the Diplomat Resort Country Club & Spa by introducing a venue for fitness, sports, and such events as weddings, corporate conferences and weekend getaways, where being smaller and more informal can be better.

Above right: Fountain and pool.
Right: *Connecting breezeways.*
Below: *A cluster of the Club's structures.*
Photography: *Ed Zealy*

Skidmore, Owings & Merrill LLP

14 Wall Street
New York
New York 10005
212.298.9300
212.298.9500 (Fax)

224 S. Michigan Avenue
Chicago
Illinois 60604
312.554.9090
312.360.4545 (Fax)

One Front Street
San Francisco
California 94111
415.981.1555
415.398.3214 (Fax)

30 Millbank
London SW1P 4SD
United Kingdom
44.20.7798.1000
44.20.7798.1100 (Fax)

www.som.com
info@som.com

Skidmore, Owings & Merrill LLP

Solana Marriott Hotel
Westlake, Texas

Left: *Registration area.*
Above: *Lounge with fireplace.*
Right: *Bar with asymmetrical cone.*
Photography: *Nick Merrick, Hedrich Blessing.*

Left: Prefunction area.
Right: Example of custom furnishings.

Where would visitors to IBM and other corporations at a 600-acre office park in Westlake, Texas like to relax after work? Creating a superior environment for them was the challenge confronting Ricardo Legoretta as exterior architect and Skidmore, Owings & Merrill as interior designer of the Solana Marriott Hotel. The hotel represents a rare and breathtaking integration of architecture and interior design. Legoretta's strong forms and vivid colors have provided a context for SOM's dazzling, 185,000-square foot Modern interior, incorporating traditional Mexican materials such as wood flooring, rough-finish plaster walls and patinated bronze trim. Consequently, the hotel's 193 rooms, six suites, 5,500-square foot ballroom, two boardrooms, restaurant, bar and living room with fireplace and baby grand piano form an oasis of uncommon tranquillity and comfort. Though references to Legoretta's visual language are visible everywhere, the interior projects a spirit of its own, using hand-crafted construction, a rich color palette, eclectic, custom-designed furniture, a variety of natural materials, custom-designed carpets and original works of art. Corporate guests can happily anticipate their evenings in Westlake.

Skidmore, Owings & Merrill LLP

Sheraton Palace Hotel
San Francisco, California

Above left: Entrance portrayed in evening view.
Above: Grand corridor with appropriate dimensions.
Left: Arcade leading to Garden Court.
Opposite: garden Court with restored skylight.
Photography: Jon Miller, Hedrich Blessing.

San Franciscans showed unmistakable pride and confidence in rebuilding the City by the Bay after the earthquake of 1906. One of the many significant buildings from their effort was the Sheraton Palace Hotel, constructed in the Beaux-Arts style in 1908 with a design by George Kelham that recalled the grand hotels and casinos of the French Riviera. Now renovated by Skidmore, Owings & Merrill, the nine-story, 550-room hotel stands as an exceptional blend of historic preservation and adaptive re-use. At the time it closed for restoration, the Sheraton Palace was virtually unchanged, allowing SOM to refurbish critical elements with historic accuracy. The 70,000-pane Garden Court skylight, for example, was meticulously dismantled and rehabilitated off-site. Yet opportunities for new functions have also been exploited, as can be seen in the new, 45,000-square foot facilities that replace additions from the 1930s with meeting rooms, a skylit pool and a health club. Equipped with such custom-designed furniture, carpets, lighting fixtures and other furnishings, the Sheraton Palace faces its second century as confidently as its first.

Skidmore, Owings & Merrill LLP

Hotel Arts Barcelona
Vila Olimpica
Barcelona, Spain

Right: Staircase.
Below left: Main lobby.
Below right: Guest tower and pool.
Photography: James H. Morris.

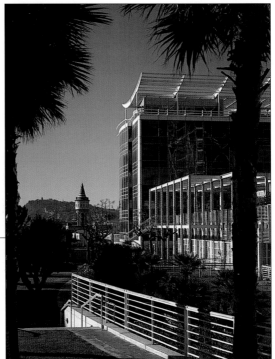

Above: Articulated structure adds to the visual distinction of the complex.
Above right: The elegant swimming pool serves health spa patrons.
Right: Guest may use the conference space in the five-story office building.
Opposite: Vila Olimpica brings hotel, office space and retail activity to the water's edge.

Sponsoring the Olympics allows host cities to dream big dreams and develop them for use during the games and after, as shown at the 1992 Summer Olympics in Barcelona. Vila Olimpica is a multi-use complex designed by Skidmore, Owings & Merrill and built on the coast of the Mediterranean Sea as part of the city's master plan for the Olympic regatta and sailing programs. Envisioned as a way to bring the city to the sea and generate a wide range of civic spaces and activities, the 109,000-square meter development includes offices, apartments and a village-like retail center along with a sleek, 456-room, five-star business hotel, the Hotel Arts. In keeping with the ambitious scheme, the hotel offers world-class business services with outstanding resort facilities. Guests can enjoy its restaurants and lounges, ballroom facilities and health club steps away from conference facilities at the nearby five-story, 12,800-square meter office building. Just a 15-minute walk from the Ramblas, the hotel and the Vila Olimpica are proud, living witnesses to the 1992 Summer Games.

Skidmore, Owings & Merrill LLP

Four Seasons Jakarta
Jakarta, Indonesia

Right: Staircase.
Below left: Main lobby.
Below right: Guest tower and pool.
Photography: James H. Morris.

For a taste of elegance, service and amenity in Southeast Asia worthy of the grand hotels of the 19th century, guests can head for the Four Seasons Jakarta, a 400-room hotel designed by Skidmore, Owings & Merrill and situated in the heart of Jakarta's central business district. Respecting a city planning envelope that capped building coverage at 40 percent and height at 16 stories, SOM has produced a central courtyard composition of low buildings, guest tower and landscaping that operate as a dignified suite of indoor and outdoor spaces. The 84,224-square meter interior includes grand public spaces, retail stores, three restaurants and bars, main ballroom and function spaces, health club and below-grade parking for 300 cars. A lush oasis set in a hot, humid city, the Four Seasons Jakarta is intended as a gathering place for the business elite, and that's how Jakarta likes it.

Smallwood, Reynolds, Stewart, Stewart & Associates, Inc.

One Piedmont Center
3565 Piedmont Road
Suite 303
Atlanta
Georgia 30305
404.233.5453
404.264.0929 (Fax)

www.srssa.com
architecture@srssa.com
interiors@srssa.com

100 South Ashley Drive, Suite 350
Tampa, Florida 33602
813.221.1226
813.228.9717 (Fax)

83 Clemenceau Avenue #14-03
UE Square
Singapore 239920
Republic of Singapore
65.835.4355
65.835.4322 (Fax)

Smallwood, Reynolds, Stewart, Stewart & Associates, Inc.

Inn and Golf Resort at Barnsley Gardens
Adairsville, Georgia

Above: Reception/registration building.
Right: A view of the cottages shows varied designs and sizes.
Photography: Gabriel Benzur.

Though the magnificent antebellum manor built by English-born cotton broker Godfrey Barnsley in Georgia's wooded Bartow County stands in ruins, guests are flocking to its landscaped grounds to visit the new, 19th-century village-style resort, Barnsley Inn and Golf Resort at Barnsley Gardens, designed by Smallwood, Reynolds, Stewart, Stewart & Associates. In a fairy tale-like story, Prince Hubertus Fugger of Bavaria and his wife, Princess Alexandra, purchased 1,300 acres of the estate, recreated its gardens in the manner of 19th-century architect Andrew Jackson Downing, and developed a "village" of 33 English-style cottages with 70 guest suites, the Rice House, a log house that is now the formal restaurant, the Pavilion, which houses a ballroom and meeting rooms, a chapel, a golf clubhouse and a spa—all fit for a prince and princess.

Right: Bathrooms convey the overall romantic theme.
Below: Gracious appointments make this bedroom glow.

267

Smallwood, Reynolds, Stewart, Stewart & Associates, Inc.

Wyndham Atlanta Hotel
Atlanta, Georgia

The upscale renovation of the facade and interiors of the 312-room Wyndham Atlanta Hotel by Smallwood, Reynolds, Stewart, Stewart & Associates acknowledges the unique character of this southern city. An elegant, new design emphasizes tradition yet incorporates the latest technologies in the HVAC, elevators and telecommunications. Bringing fresh ideas to guestrooms, ballrooms, meeting rooms, restaurant, lobby and pool area, the designers let guests revel in the new interior scheme, tinted in deep reds, blues and chocolates, as they connect their laptops to the Internet.

Top: Southern comfort reigns in the two-story lobby lounge.
Above: The restaurant introduces a distinctive new character.
Right: A traditional image is newly created for the facade.
Photography: Gabriel Benzur.

Smallwood, Reynolds, Stewart, Stewart & Associates, Inc.

AT&T Conference Center
Basking Ridge, New Jersey

Right: Guestrooms place corporate students "at home."
Below: A suite.
Photography: Robert Miller.

Continuing education is a fact of life in the Information Age, but today's corporate conference and training center does a lot more than promote the three R's. The interior design of the 166,000-square foot AT&T Conference Center in Basking Ridge, New Jersey, by Smallwood, Reynolds, Stewart, Stewart & Associates demonstrates how critical the learning environment can be in producing a superior educational experience for the business world. The design of the executive-style conference and training facilities, hotel-like hospitality complex and 175 residential-style guestrooms not only respects the wooded, hilly countryside where the building stands across the road from AT&T's corporate headquarters, it acknowledges the physical and social needs of the participants. The Center welcomes you to learn.

Smallwood, Reynolds, Stewart, Stewart & Associates, Inc.

Westin Harbor Resort
Savannah, Georgia

Given the feelings we harbor for our mothers, it's easy to see how Georgians regard Savannah. The "Mother City of Georgia," Savannah was the state's first colonial settlement, built to a design by founder James Oglethorpe and William Bull. Citizens have taken great care since the 1950s to restore and maintain the old buildings in the port city's original settlement area, producing a spectacular historic district that has attracted tourists since the early 1980s. The same concern can be seen in the new 403-room Westin Harbor Resort, designed by Smallwood, Reynolds, Stewart, Stewart & Associates and located on reclaimed land directly across the Savannah River from the historic waterfront. To blend the resort's architecture with old Savannah, the designers have employed elements common to the city's Regency style, such as bay windows, lunette

windows, stucco detailing and deeply articulated arched openings. Inside, the theme is carried through with an interior design that combines Savannah's proud design heritage, the bright, cheery color palette common to William Jay's houses, dramatic lighting and state-of-the-art guest services. The Westin's guests are delighted—as Mother would surely be.

Above: *A gracious, Regency-style facade acknowledges historic Savannah.*
Left: *Respect for history joins the lobby lounge to old Savannah.*
Opposite page: *A restaurant.*
Photography: *Scott McDonald© Hedrich Blessing.*

Smallwood, Reynolds, Stewart, Stewart & Associates, Inc.

Grande Lakes Resort
Orlando, Florida

West Bay Complex and Four Seasons Hotel
Doha, Qatar

In a marriage of corporate siblings, a 25-story, 980,000-square foot Marriott and a 15-story, 635,000-square foot Ritz-Carlton will share the same spa, health club and golf club, while projecting separate identities to their guests at the Grande Lakes Resort in Orlando, Florida. The design, by Smallwood, Reynolds, Stewart, Stewart & Associates, portrays the Marriott as a grand hotel in the early 1900s tradition, while the Ritz-Carlton honors celebrated architect Addison Mizner, whose buildings epitomized the Roaring Twenties. Guests will be dazzled by the design, but hoteliers will marvel at the efficiency and economy of scale.

Left: *Guests arriving at Grande Lakes Resort are met by one of two hotels whose shared facilities present two distinctly different architectural images.*
Below: *Tradition meets high technology in Doha.*

The West-Bay Complex is a 1.5 million sq.ft. mixed-use development by the Arabian Gulf in Doha. The components of the project include: a 240-key, 18-story Four Seasons Resort Hotel and Club with a grotto resort pool and pool bar. A 30-story office building; two 20-story luxury apartment buildings; and a full-service marina. In Qatar, there was not a history of high-rise buildings. So, extensive research was undertaken into the historic architecture of Qatar in developing an appropriate contemporary aesthetic.

Sue Firestone & Associates

5383 Hollister Avenue

Suite 140

Santa Barbara

California 93111

805.692.1948

805.692.9293 (Fax)

www.sfadesign.com

Sue Firestone & Associates

Disney's BoardWalk Inn
Lake Buena Vista, Florida

Left: The Presidential Suite offers spacious comfort.
Below left: A view of the Vacation Club lobby.
Below right: Inside the glamorous Atlantic Ballroom.
Opposite: Main lobby features "Elephant Hotel" and roller coaster models.
Photography: Robert Miller.

Located on Crescent Lake, is the 45-acre Disney's BoardWalk Inn, in Walt Disney World, Lake Buena Vista, Florida. Here guests visit one of America's colorful early 20th-century seaside resorts. There are fanciful boardwalk buildings designed by Robert A.M. Stern Architects that house restaurants, retail shops and entertainment venues. For guests of the resort's 393-room Disney's BoardWalk Inn or one of 532 villas at Disney Vacation Club, there are also a double-height lobby, lounges and sitting areas, guestrooms, suites and a 15,000-square foot conference center, all handsomely designed and appointed by Sue Firestone & Associates. The image of America circa 1900 is captured by such details as wicker furniture, custom, period-inspired textiles, white oak floors bordered by green granite, large potted palms and a wonderful collection of period accessories. Come to think of it, maybe you can smell the salty air if you really try.

Sue Firestone & Associates

Indian Wells Country Club
Indian Wells, California

Above: *This rustic yet elegant lounge says welcome to Indian Wells.*

Affluent, sophisticated and lively Indian Wells, just two hours from Los Angeles, is one of southern California's most desirable getaways for golf, tennis and the good life. Amidst its striking desert environment are such attractions as the Bob Hope Chrysler Classic for golf pros and celebrity players, the Masters Tennis Series at the new Indian Wells Tennis Garden, the extraordinary Desert Town Hall Lecture Series featuring such dignitaries as George Bush and Lady Margaret Thatcher, and a full calendar of performing arts. A choice vantage point to enjoy everything is the Indian Wells Country Club. In its 60,000-square foot interiors are public spaces, banquet facilities, men's and women's lounges and other rustic yet elegant accommodations designed by Sue Firestone & Associates with such distinctive furnishings as Spanish Mission-inspired furniture, dramatic lighting fixtures and textured fabrics. It's a perfect setting to begin or end a day in this desert paradise.

Sue Firestone & Associates

Park Wilshire
Los Angeles, California

Outstanding model units are as indispensable to multi-unit residential property sales as provocative covers are to bookselling in today's competitive marketplace. A perfect textbook example of how this works is the recently completed Park Wilshire, a luxury high-rise residence in Los Angeles, where the model units and such public spaces as the entry lobby, lounge and banquet facilities have been planned and designed by Sue Firestone & Associates. The design firm was retained when a previous effort by another design firm failed to communicate the Park Wilshire's potential style, comfort and livability to prospective customers— a particularly formidable challenge in a region that is better known for single family detached homes. New floor plans characterized by utility, efficiency and grace were drawn up by the designers as the basis for an interior design of classic, International-style aesthetic refinement. The result? Sales took off once the new model units opened.

Top: A view of the stylishly appointed lobby.
Above: One of the luxurious model living rooms.
Right: The banquet room is available to residents.

277

Sue Firestone & Associates

Sonoma Mission Inn & Spa
Sonoma, California

Right: A typical court-
yard entrance.
Below left: *The spa
veranda.*
Below right: *A view of
the outdoor bathing
sequence.*
Photography: *Courtesy
of Sonoma Mission Inn &
Spa.*

How do you embellish a venerable, high-end and much-loved inn to serve growing numbers of guests in the heart of California's wine country--without jeopardizing its heritage? For the Sonoma Mission Inn & Spa, the best course has been to develop yet another addition. Most recently, the Inn developed 30,500 square feet of expanded spa, remodeled bathhouse and 30 new suites with an interior design by Sue Firestone & Associates. While guests will remain blissfully unaware of the design problems faced by the design firm in producing the new facilities, which have been given rave reviews by both guests and travel editors, the new construction skillfully reconciles diverse cultural themes.

First, the Inn's existing California Mission style is romantically sustained as its signature image in the new suites. Then, the Inn introduces sleek, Romanesque and high-tech elements in the expanded spa and remodeled bathhouse, acknowledging the Roman origins of the Inn's new sequence of pools from cold to hot, which the owners have admired in European spas. Adapting to the times is nothing new for the Inn, however. It traces its origin as a resort to a day in 1895 when Captain H.E. Boyes acquired the property and struck 112-degree mineral water at a depth of 70 feet while drilling a well. Within five years, Boyes had opened his Boyes Hot Spring Hotel and lured affluent San

Above: Spa lounge.
Right: Indoor bathing pool.

279

Franciscans to "take the waters." The current Inn dates from 1927, when a new building took the place of its predecessor, lost to a fire four years before, and opened its doors as the Sonoma Mission Inn. The Inn would change hands a number of times more—including a stint as a Navy "R&R" site for sailors during World War II—prior to its revival in 1980 in the spirit of the Inn of 1927.

With a revitalized design, added space and enhanced amenities, the Inn should easily persuade new generations of guests to "take the waters."

Vision Design, Inc.

500 Crescent Court

Suite 300

Dallas, Texas 75201

214.871.4777

214.871.4788 (Fax)

dan_nelson@rosewd.com

Vision Design, Inc.

Hotel La Samanna
St. Martin, French West Indies

Just thinking about resorts like La Samanna on St. Martin in the French West Indies, inspired by turn-of-the-century French-Moroccan architecture, can stimulate our imagination the way movies like "The Road to Morocco" and "Casablanca" did over a half century ago. Thus, to develop three suites at the 83-room hotel, Vision Design, Inc. capitalized on the wealth of imagery in the original structure to create a distinctive new design. All furnishings were produced specifically for

Above: *Furniture ensemble with whimsical rockers.*
Above right: *A living room with a sweeping ocean view.*
Right: *Handcrafted furnishings draw on many cultures.*
Photography: *Mike Wilson*

Right: *Elegant bath counter featuring hand-carved legs.*
Below: *Dining area brings the outdoors inside.*

the suites, and showed evidence of Moroccan and North African sources, as well as the sophistication of Art Moderne, a style that flourished in France, and the Afro-Cubist art of Constantin Brancusi and Pierre Legrain. Fabrication techniques were contrasted to dramatic effect so hand-carved elements would play off modern machined lines in furniture of teak, mahogany, bamboo and metal, English hand-printed fabrics would form lush tableaux with hand-made batiks and ikats from Indonesia and the Philippines, pristine, bowl-like sinks would be foils for hand-painted ceramic tiles, and TV's, VCR's, stereos and other electronic accessories would hide, ready to pop up from bed-benches. No wonder this project, recent winner of the coveted Gold Key Award, is turning the heads of even the most jaded travelers.

Vision Design, Inc.

The Mansion on Turtle Creek
Dallas, Texas

Right: Living room in a suite.
Below left: Typical new bathroom.
Below right: Bedroom with canopy.
Photography: Ira Montgomery

We may never know how Renaissance aristocrat Lorenzo de' Medici felt upon arising each day in his Florentine palazzo, but there was certainly nothing conjectural about creating a sumptuous experience for guests of The Mansion on Turtle Creek, the acclaimed, five-star luxury hotel in Dallas. When Vision Design, Inc. was asked to refurbish and update 11 suites and to remodel the public spaces and restaurant in the structure adjacent to the Sheppard King Mansion, built in the Italian Renaissance style by oil and cotton magnate Sheppard King in 1925, the goal was to give the facilities the ambiance of a private residence. To comply, the designers drew on the celebrated

Right: *Lobby lounge detail.*
Below: *A welcoming view of the restaurant.*

oilman's history and residence to create a signature style of uncommon residential warmth. Although the project honored its set budget, such extravagant materials and furnishings as Spanish style desks, rich leather upholstery, stone moldings, bedroom canopies, brass nailheads and original works of art were strategically installed within the various spaces, while stylish but less costly equivalents were employed elsewhere. Thus, even the public spaces and restaurant displayed the same high level of finish as the suites without exacting undue costs. How de' Medici might have regarded all this will always be a mystery, but it's easy to imagine "Il Magnifico" expressing his approval.

Vision Design, Inc.

Caneel Bay Hotel
St. John, U.S. Virgin Islands

Below left: Lobby lounge area.
Bottom left: Guestroom with four-poster.
Right: Starlight Terrace.
Photography: Mike Wilson

After a hurricane damaged Caneel Bay Hotel in St. John, U.S. Virgin Islands, Vision Design, Inc. was invited to restore the classic Caribbean resort originally developed by Laurance Rockefeller in the 1950s. Because the designers were also encouraged to update the hotel's appeal to a new generation of guests, they began by conducting extensive research into motifs, materials and colors holding historic and contemporary significance. Guestrooms received new and often custom designed furnishings as a consequence, incorporating indigenous bamboo, mahogany and rattan. The restaurants, including chef Dean Fearing's signature Equator, received such improvements as fresh finishes, custom designed furnishings and a new cookline buffet. Public areas saw new furnishings and finishes. Subsequent increases in the hotel's restaurant and room revenues as well as overall occupancy offer welcome reassurance that guests love this classic more than ever.

Right: Custom rattan furniture graces guestroom.
Below: Beach Terrace Restaurant & Bar with new rotisserie-style buffet.

Vision Design, Inc.

The Bristol Panama
Panama City, Panama

Above: *Guest services amidst local art and craftsmanship.*
Left: *Restaurant and bar salute the Canal era, 1882-1914.*
Below: *A guestroom fit for the global traveler.*
Photography: *Mike Wilson*

Even without knowing how the Panama Canal was constructed from 1882-1914, no one can observe ships navigating the towering Gaillard Cut without appreciating the effort it required. This key chapter of Panama's history became an obvious inspiration for the recent design of The Bristol, a five-star, 57-room, 100,000-square foot luxury hotel in Panama City by Vision Design, Inc., particularly in the restaurant and bar. An international flavor characterizes guestrooms and public spaces, reflecting guests arriving from all over the world. However, the design also celebrates the region's personality through its craftsmen and materials. Local cabinetmakers made the custom-designed case-goods, for example, while local sculptors carved stone lamp bases, Central American artisans fabricated cast iron furniture, Panamanian Indian weavers prepared "mola" textiles for guest-room pillows, and Panamanian and South American artists provided original works of art. It's a compelling vision of Panama's place in the world.

Wimberly
Allison
Tong &
Goo

700 Bishop Street
Suite 1800
Honolulu
Hawaii 96813
808.521.8888
808.521.3888 (Fax)
honolulu@watg.com

Alexandra House
6 Little Portland Street
London W1W 1JE
England
44 (0) 207.906.6600
44 (0) 207.906.6660 (Fax)
london@watg.com

2260 University Drive
Newport Beach
California 92660
949.574.8500
947.574.8550 (Fax)
newport@watg.com

37A Cuppage Road
Singapore 229460
65.277.2618
65.227.0650 (Fax)
singapore@watg.com

Wimberly Allison Tong & Goo

Atlantis, Paradise Island
Bahamas

Right: Voyagers restaurant, just off the casino floor.
Below: Rotunda, sized on the grand Atlantis scale.
Photography: Courtesy Sun International.

Whether or not the legendary city of Atlantis existed, its modern counterpart has been thriving on Paradise Island, Bahamas, since Sun International embarked on its ambitious renovation and expansion a few years ago with Wimberly Allison Tong & Goo. Phase I saw the restoration and modernization of a 75-room luxury hotel and the creation of new restaurants and bars for over 1,000 guests, renovated and new public spaces, redevelopment of 14 acres of amenities and beachfront, and back of house modernization. Phase II, encompassing 1.4 million square feet and 30 acres, has been no less dynamic, adding such new facilities as two 23-story, sky bridge-linked hotel towers with 1,202 rooms, a casino, a ballroom, 11 meeting rooms, seven restaurants, five lounges and six bars. What has tripled revenue per room is the imaginative way the design incorporates elements of marine life, the Caribbean setting and ancient cultures such as the Mayans into an architectural context that is highly functional, visually spellbinding and far more comfortable than any earlier Atlantis could be.

Above: The new marina with casino, restaurants and retail to the right and the Royal Towers in the background.
Right: Dining beneath a barrel vaulted ceiling in the Great Hall of Waters.

Wimberly Allison Tong & Goo

Mövenpick Dead Sea Resort
Dead Sea, Jordan

Right: The resort emulates a Jordanian village with its interconnected buildings.
Above right: Guestrooms offer traditional style and comfort for extended stays.
Below: Arabic art, architecture and interior design motifs enrich the lobby lounge.
Photography: Ken Kirkwood.

Left: Refined architectural motifs and graceful furnishings characterize the entire facility.
Below: All resort structures are handsomely integrated into the sloping, boulder-strewn site.

Does the lowest spot on earth maintain the highest standards of luxury? That's the impression guests have of the Mövenpick Dead Sea Resort in Jordan, designed by Wimberly Allison Tong & Goo. Luring tourists from established seaside destinations in Israel and Egypt was the not inconsiderable goal of the 232-room, five-star, world class facility. The elevation, 1,320 feet (400 meters) below sea level, assures that there is virtually no ultraviolet radiation to cause sunburn. But the architecture seizes the initiative with its vision of a Jordanian village. Its ornate main building and numerous ancillary structures, including restaurants, shops, artisan workshops and a courtyard, are carefully integrated into a sloping, boulder-strewn site. Guests can savor details drawn from Arabic art and interpreted with local materials in spaces ranging from spacious guestrooms, each with its own, shaded private terrace, to the Sanctuary Zara Spa, one of the most sophisticated in the Middle East. Whether hydrotherapy and 60 other spa treatments or a milieu reminiscent of old Jerusalem prompted *Conde Nast Traveler's* recent praise, this Dead Sea Resort is very much alive.

Wimberly Allison Tong & Goo

Four Seasons Resort
Punta Mita
Nayarit, Mexico

How do you place 110 guestrooms and 21 suites on a pristine and spectacular 1,700-acre coastal site in Nayarit, Mexico, without marring the scale and beauty of the land? For Wimberly Allison Tong & Goo, the solution has been to house the Four Seasons Resort Punta Mita in 13 casitas and other buildings one to three stories tall, conceived in a style inspired by the vernacular in the neighboring states of Valisco and Nayarit. The resulting "village," complete with a fitness center, spa, two restaurants, meeting room, kid's club and pool, is radiant with such indigenous finishing touches as stucco walls, clay barrel roof tiles and stone paving tile floors. Yet fine as the guestrooms, public areas and outdoor facilities are, with commensurate interiors, they make no attempt to overpower the natural splendor around them. Accordingly, *Travel & Leisure* calls the resort "one of the best trips for the 21st century."

Above: Exterior in vernacular form.
Below left: Guestroom with ocean view.
Photography: Mary E. Nichols.

Above: Rustic doors serve as foils for a modern setting.
Opposite: A soaring roof shelters a gracious lounge.

Wimberly Allison Tong & Goo

Padovani's Bistro & Wine Bar
Honolulu, Hawaii

Left: *Downstairs dining room.*
Below: *Restaurant Cruvinet system.*
Photography: *Rothenborg Pacific.*

Mention "Old Hawaii" to older Islanders, and you conjure a romantic, elegant yet relaxed era from the 1930s to 1950s. That's what Wimberly Allison Tong & Goo sought in designing Padovani's Bistro & Wine Bar in Honolulu. In just four months, it transformed an existing restaurant through added "curb appeal," updated kitchen and building systems, raised ceilings with soffits, and a new interior design. The 70-seat downstairs dining room and 40-seat upstairs wine bar of Padovani's are resplendent with design elements from East and West, sensuous materials like polished wood, etched glass, custom lighting, fine fabrics and carpet, and a color scheme of gold, jade green and mahogany. Happily, nobody is too young to miss this glorious "Old Hawaii."

FUCSIA by Achille Castiglioni

FLOSUSA

1 800 939 3567   1 631 549 2745

By Roger Yee

What Does Today's Guest Want?

Vanilla, chocolate and strawberry are no longer enough. Giving 21st century customers more and better choices is quickening business competition throughout the global economy. Who hasn't noticed how the Internet became more than an intellectual curiosity when the public discovered an alternative to retail stores called Amazon.com, an electronic rival to flea markets called eBay and a 24-hour way to chat called America Online? The highly competitive hospitality industry, which embraces restaurants as well as hotels, knows the impact of proliferating choices firsthand as it enters the 21st century. Finding the right combination of food and/or lodging service and physical environment to satisfy today's guest is serious business for the $358-billion U.S. restaurant industry (1999 total sales are courtesy of the National Restaurant Association) and the $93.1-billion U.S. lodging industry (1998 total sales are courtesy of the American Hotel & Motel Association).

Business is good—very good—for hospitality. Nearly half of all adults in America (46 percent) patronized restaurants on a typical day in 1998. For 1997, travelers in the United States spent an average of $1.41 billion a day on lodging, transportation, food service and more.

Not every restaurateur, hotelier or operator of a spa, country club, convention center or other hospitality-related business will prosper, however, even amidst the prodigious wealth of the New Economy. Customers simply have too many choices to have to settle for anything less than they want. The "right" combination of food and/or lodging, service and physical environment depends on who is being served.

Everyone wants good value—the poor out of necessity and the rich on principle. But are you talking about top-of-the-line luxury or no-frills bargains? Service can be provided by an army of maitre d'hôtel's, concierges, butlers, maids, porters and doormen, or a single, well-equipped, do-it-yourself guest. Food and beverage may easily range from a tender filet mignon and a glass of merlot to a slice of pizza and a can of soda. As for the physical environment or what is often referred to as "the box" or "decor," it can deliberately place you in the real or simulated heart of a palazzo or the generic equivalent of a government office with a dining table or a bed.

> *B*usiness is good—very good—for hospitality. Nearly half of all adults in America (46 percent) patronized restaurants on a typical day in 1998. For 1997, travelers in the United States spent an average of $1.41 billion a day on lodging, transportation, food service and more.

© Copyright 2000, Hansgrohe, Inc.

Phoenix Design

Philippe Starck

Masterpieces of Design and Function.

AXOR®
hansgrohe

800.719.1000
www.hansgrohe-usa.com

All this matters more than before because the global economy and information technology are evolving so rapidly that customers have more money and less time to spend, know what is available simultaneously elsewhere, and expect more of the hospitality experience at every price point. Whether the mission supporting the transaction is business or leisure, today's guest can afford to be remarkably choosy about satisfying his or her personal needs, so that winning the business becomes a battle of brands, products, people and real estate. Consider some of the recent trends in the U.S. restaurant and hotel industries that are outlined here.

Restaurants keep consuming more of the food budget

Restaurateurs have good reason to be optimistic about their long-term future. Americans love dining out and show no sign of losing their appetite. The National Restaurant Association predicts that U.S. sales will rise by 5 percent in 2000 to set an industry record of $376 billion—representing over 45 percent of the American food dollar.

*F*ull-service restaurants have been undergoing a renaissance in recent years, with revenue gains estimated at 33 percent for 1996-2000, as Americans used their growing income to indulge a new appetite for the more sophisticated tastes and customized menus.

In fact, the association forecasts that the restaurant industry will become the leading purveyor of food in the nation by 2010, pulling ahead of such dominant vendors as supermarkets to capture 53 percent of each food dollar. Recent research by the association reveals that almost half or 48 percent of adults agree that restaurants are an important part of their lifestyle. Getting more specific, nearly two out of five, or 39 percent, say that using restaurants allows them to be more productive, and almost nine out of 10, or 88 percent, believe that eating at restaurants is usually fun.

Why has dining out become almost an entitlement in America? Again, the circumstances vary with the customers. Examine the impact of work and child rearing, for example. Changing household demographics point to a rising number of two-income families with children, 17 percent, and working married couples without children, 13 percent, who indicate that dining offers them convenience, saves time and provides a pleasurable experience.

Interestingly enough, restaurant going cuts across generational lines. Although Baby Boomers are at the peak of their earning years, and have established themselves as loyal restaurant customers, the generations following them are cultivating a taste for dining out as well. Generation has been depicted in consumer research as maturing later, feeling insecure and placing a high value on leisure activities and entertainment, while Generation is portrayed as maturing earlier, leading regimented lives and lacking free time. As different as these generations appear to be, they both see restaurant going in a favorable light.

GASSER SEATING

IS THE FIRST

CHOICE OF MANY

FINE HOTELS,

RESTAURANTS

AND RESORTS.

The Biltmore Hotel
Coral Gables, Florida

Leylaty Ballroom
Jeddah, Saudi Arabia

Only the Finest... *...Quality Seating*

SINCE 1946

GASSER CHAIR COMPANY, INC.

4136 LOGANWAY • YOUNGSTOWN, OH 44505

800 752 9318 • FAX 330.759.9844

WWW.GASSERCHAIR.COM

Why full service is outpacing fast food

The food service industry has adapted to the diverging scenarios of its customers by giving them a wide array of dining formats, from fast food and table service to freshly prepared or frozen foods that can be enjoyed at home. In a surprising reversal of trends, full-service restaurants have been undergoing a renaissance in recent years, with revenue gains estimated at 33 percent for 1996 to 2000, as Americans used their growing income to indulge a new appetite for the more sophisticated tastes and customized menus that both moderately priced and fine-dining establishments are equipped to satisfy, outpacing the gains scored by fast-food restaurants, which are expected to reach 23 percent for the same period.

*R*estaurants seem to be calling in architects and interior designers at every price point. In the same 1999 study of "Tableservice" and "Quickservice" operators by the Association, nearly half of the former and three quarters of the latter made capital expenditures for remodeling.

What may adversely affect the industry's ability to provide good service to its growing clientele is its labor supply. Facing the lowest unemployment rates in years, restaurant operators around the nation have told the National Restaurant Association that finding qualified and motivated workers from its primary labor pool of 16- to 24-year-olds is a major challenge in 2000. This demographic segment is growing again after declining in the early 1990s, but demand is likely to keep outpacing supply. Thus, restaurant operators have focused on employee recruitment and retention by raising employee satisfaction through more training, employee recognition and financial incentives. Customers can readily tell whether a restaurant's staff is providing good service or not, and poor training and frequent turnover would quickly cost more money over the long run than they could possibly save.

Chances are today's restaurants will benefit from the added attention to employees as much as the employees themselves, particularly as technology plays an expanding role in enhancing efficiency and productivity. Computer systems that can routinely tell restaurateurs what is selling, at what price and at what time of the day, week or year, what their expenses and revenues are at a given moment, and other vital financial facts are best managed by properly trained staff. The role of PCs in food service is already so well established that a 1999 study by the association showed 60 percent of respondents to its Tableservice Operator Survey and 70 percent of respondents to its Quickservice Operator Survey credit PCs with making their businesses more efficient.

Do food and entertainment still mix?

Besides setting a bountiful table with the right food and beverage at a fair price, and employing workers who want to serve with distinction, restaurateurs are also

Project :
lagio
sign Firm:
DA Designs Inc., NJ

S I R M O S

CORPORATE HEADQUARTERS 30-00 FORTY-SEVENTH AVENUE, LONG ISLAND CITY, NY 11101-3146
T 718.786.5920   F 718.482.9402   EMAIL corp@sirmos.com

Project:
is Hotel Resort & Casino
& Associates,TX

Project:
Atlantis Hotel Resort & Casino
Design Firm:
Wilson & Associates,TX

Project:
Farralon Restaurant
Designer:
Pat Kuleto

Project:
Atlantis Hotel Resort & Casino
Design Firm:
Wilson & Associates,TX

Project:
Cheesecake Factory
Designer:
Rick Mc Cormick/Cheesecake Factory

Project:
Atlantis Hotel Resort & Casino
Design Firm:
Wilson & Associates,TX

responding to rising customer expectations by remodeling the front of the house to introduce more visual interest, stronger architectural elements and perhaps a sense of "fun." What's encouraging for the design community is that restaurants seem to be calling in architects and interior designers at every price point. In the same 1999 study of "Tableservice" and "Quickservice" operators by the association, nearly half of the former and three quarters of the latter made capital expenditures for remodeling.

How does today's best-dressed dining room look? Whether the business in question is a fast-food giant such as Burger King, which intends to overhaul its entire chain in the next few years, or an exquisite, family-owned, fine dining establishment in a major metropolitan area, there is no particular aesthetic trend to discern. Restaurant interiors can be more or less theatrical, particularly if their menus focus on specific ethnic cuisines, such as Italian, Thai or Mexican, or genres of American cooking, such as barbecue, seafood or steaks and chops, but the emphasis today is on appropriateness.

The theme- and entertainment-oriented restaurants that were the rage just a few years ago may or may not have reached the limit of their appeal in the new century, but they no longer seem destined to take over the food service industry. Just because dining out has often become the source of an afternoon or evening's entertainment does not mean that the decor must grab guests by their senses and hold their attention. People clearly consider an appealing environment to be essential to the restaurant experience, however, so the challenge to restaurateurs is to match their food and service with the right architecture and interior design.

Hotels that follow customers everywhere

Numerous as the latest crop of full-service restaurants may be, they must still emerge from the shadow of expanding food service giants, as fast-food icons such as McDonald's, Burger King, Wendy's, Pizza Hut and Taco Bell, and family and casual dining chains enlarge their franchises by growing internally and acquiring other food-service businesses. Industry consolidation is also a fact of life in the innkeeping business. Hilton, Marriott, Four Seasons, Starwood and other chains continue to extend their rule over key markets around the world through new product development and acquisition, while smaller companies are combining to form larger ones.

The recent shift in emphasis by major hotel operators from acquisition to reorganization through the sale of non-core assets, reduction of debt and more effective management of portfolios does not alter the general perception that a global reach has become essential for success. Hoteliers can readily identify the benefits of size: economies of scale, leverage in reservation systems, lowered entry level costs in new markets and so on. In other words, size matters.

Of course, being everywhere that customers need you to be makes sense only when customers know who you are, what you stand for, and why you should be their preferred innkeeper. Marketing is key to success in the lodging industry today. As Roger Hill, president of The Gettys Group, a leading hotel consultant, explains, hotels must take care in differentiating their products in meaningful ways from those of competitors, achieving a level of brand standardization that gives their customers

In the Seat of the Night.

Union League Club
Chicago, Illinois

"I'm positive, Constable,"
the wine steward insisted,
"I last saw the unfortunate
woman draped languidly
in that chair near the window."
"Fascinating," Constable
Hemlock replied, tugging
at his handlebar moustache.
"Fascinating in that
you now have some insight
into Miss Cumberfort's
mysterious disappearance?"
asked the steward. "No,"
Hemlock replied, peering
through his monocle.
"Fascinating in the sense that
anyone could bear to abandon
that exquisite chair."

The 95/1 Salon Side Chair
from the MTS Banquet and
Stackable Seating Collection

Style, comfort, performance,
value. For the whole story,
call us at 734-847-3875 or
visit us at www.mtsseating.com.

Seating's only half the story.

©2000 MTS Seating

what they expect when they check in, yet offering them conveniences, amenities and options that are based on knowing their needs in every local market. It pays to be constantly alert to change, Hill adds. While the requirements of business travelers and leisure travelers are obviously not alike, for example, they are converging in some unexpected ways.

Like home in ways we never imagined

Boasts about frequent-flier mileage notwithstanding, even hardened road warriors in the business community are increasingly asking for a more home-like environment in their hotels. Many hoteliers are responding to this sentiment by acknowledging the locations of their properties with enriched local content. Inviting local craftsmen and artists to contribute to the physical environment of the hotel, and incorporating local historical and contemporary cultural motifs may seem like superficial gestures coming from international hotel operators, but the anonymous nature of many hotel interiors cries out for some connection to the real world outside their doors.

Another way that hotels can acquire a more domestic image is to include smaller and more intimately detailed facilities that break with the generic restaurants (or non-existent restaurants), bland function areas, neglected exercise/fitness rooms and predictable gift shops that guests so frequently encounter. One type of facility that Hill has found to be very well received is a cozy library for quiet dinners where guests can dine comfortably in groups or alone, with or without bringing their work along, a welcome alternative for those who do not leave the hotel for dinner and socializing, as is commonly assumed. Still, this yearning for domesticity does not prevent the same business travelers from demanding more telephone lines, fax and copier services, laptop computers, Internet links, and other information services in their guestrooms.

> *I*nterestingly, a profound yearning for domesticity does not prevent veteran business travelers—"road warriors"—from demanding more telephone lines, facsimile and copier services, laptop computers, Internet links, and other information services in their guestrooms.

Paradoxically, computers do allow hotels big and small to add a homey, personal touch to guest services by honoring repeat customers' preferences through simple. computer-based guest tracking. Do you have allergies that require special precautions? Are there certain foods or beverages that should be stocked in the kitchenette? Would you like to listen to classical or jazz CDs whenever possible? Thanks to the relatively inexpensive cost of today's information technology, bed and breakfast inns can offer the same personal attention to guests as international hotel operators.

But a new phenomenon of business travel is raising the concept of the hotel as a home away from home to new heights: families traveling on combined business and leisure trips. Time-pressed Baby Boomer and Generation X families, no

Clubs,

Offices,

Lobbies,

Casinos,

Ballrooms,

Foodcourts,

Restaurants,

Guestrooms,

Conference Centers,

everyday, at work or at play . . .

SHELBY WILLIAMS

"CHANGING THE WAY THE WORLD SITS"™

150 Shelby Williams Drive • Morristown, TN 37813 • Phone: 423.586.7000 • Fax: 423.586.2260 • E-mail: shelby@usit.net • Web: www.shelbywilliams.com

© 2000 by Shelby Williams Industries, Inc.

longer able to count on the long summer vacations that once put entire households on the road for weeks at a time, now take shorter vacations of three to four days at a stretch whenever and wherever opportunities present themselves. In the newly integrated world of work and play, Saturday is becoming the most heavily booked night of the week, as a family that spends Wednesday, Thursday and Friday apart, so that a parent can participate in a training or sales meeting, is reunited for recreation.

Mixing official business and family pleasure has had unforeseen effects on hotels that once focused mainly on giving business travelers all the convention-size grand ballrooms, meeting rooms, formal restaurants and business services they routinely request. Now, putting in luxurious spas as well as fitness centers and developing children's recreation or amusement areas with genuine play value make hotels more appealing to spouses and families contemplating weekend stays. Operators that have prided themselves on making their facilities and experiences more enjoyable for women and senior citizens are already finding creative ways to turn young families into satisfied, steady customers.

Guests at all room rates have benefited from recent enhancements in architecture, interior design, FF&E (furnishings, fixtures and equipment), building services and on-site amenities. In fact, the distinctions between boutique hotels and their larger rivals are progressively blurring.

Smiling lips on tighter ships

Unbeknownst to many guests, hotels have tightened their operations dramatically over the last decade. What was a breakeven point of around 70 percent occupancy is now close to 50 percent. How has this been accomplished? The hotel work force, while always a major component of operating costs, has been reduced through greater efficiency in its deployment, while facilities and services are being designed to require less energy, maintenance and personnel.

Plenty of opportunities remain to create greater efficiency and value for customers, operators concede. Take the handling of a guest's arrival. Why can't a single hotel employee armed with a personal digital assistant such as a Palm Pilot take a guest straight from a curb-side check-in to a guestroom without the standard, costly, time-consuming delay at a registration desk? Numerous back-of-the-house activities can also be streamlined and automated, new energy management systems can accurately match ongoing consumption to changing occupancy conditions, new property management systems can provide faster night audits, hotel furnishings can be specified, ordered and delivered in less time and at lower cost than most suppliers now take, and so on.

In addition, hotels are discovering that they can respond more effectively to their guests' needs for food services by shifting upscale or downmarket toward fine dining or fast food in place of the standard,

EXQUISITELY BEAUTIFUL, ASTONISHINGLY REALISTIC, YET WONDERFULLY PRACTICAL.

NO LIGHT, NO WATER, NO BUGS, NO WORRIES.

THE QUALITY LEADERS IN PRESERVED AND REPLICA TREES

Call 1-800-527-8884   www.treescapes.com

PRESERVED

TREESCAPES INTERNATIONAL

4039 Avenida de la Plata, Oceanside, CA 92056 • U.S.A. Tel (800) 527-8884 / (760) 631-6789 Fax: (760) 631-6780
Offices: Chicago, Illinois • Fort Lauderdale, Florida • Scottsdale, Arizona • West Yorkshire, England • Sydney, Australia • Singapore

generic coffeeshop. Sometimes a better solution is to get out of the food service business altogether by inviting professional restaurateurs or national chains to run concessions that appeal to a wider public than the guests alone. In any event, guests who want a four-star restaurant go out of their way to make reservations at the four-star Lespinasse in Manhattan's St. Regis Hotel, while those who desire nothing more than a slice of pizza and a soda don't mind ordering from a nearby Pizza Hut that delivers to their Day's Inn.

> *T*here will always be some guests who feel more comfortable in larger, full-service branches of established global hotel chains, while others will consciously choose smaller, limited-service and frequently idiosyncratic hotels under local management and ownership. That's what the hospitality business is all about.

Precisely what constitutes a boutique hotel is debatable. A signature hip look, small size and personal service with an attitude, as defined in the 1990s by such hotels as the Triton in San Francisco, the Royalton in New York, the Mondrian in Los Angeles and the Delano in Miami Beach, have come to spell "boutique" for a young, affluent and fashion-forward crowd. Thus, operators as diverse as Ian Schrager, William Kimpton and Starwood are among those devising new game plans to capture more of these desirable customers.

Good design for every guest?

For all the economies being squeezed out of the conventional hotel, good design appears to be burgeoning everywhere. As a result of both the competitive pressures on innkeeping worldwide and the democratization of designed-oriented goods and services as they enter mass markets, the public has come to expect good design regardless of the particular market niche in question. Guests at all room rates have subsequently benefited from enhancements in architecture, interior design, FF&E (furnishings, fixtures and equipment), building services and on-site amenities. One of the more fascinating outcomes of this growing appreciation of design is the recent blurring of distinctions between boutique hotels and their larger rivals.

Schrager, whose reputation as a hotelier was firmly established by a series of intimate, ultra chic and wildly successful facilities produced with French architect Philippe Starck, is developing substantially bigger properties. Kimpton, a shrewd hotelier who has acquired and transformed ailing, small to mid-size establishments by giving them fresh new identities, has branded the Monaco name with the help of designer Cheryl Rowley and begun a nationwide roll-out. Starwood, the world's largest hotel operator, unveiled its own, sleek version of a boutique hotel as a global brand, the W, without a trace of irony just a couple of years ago.

Is the boutique phenomenon facing vast, untapped potential? Will conventional operators take selected boutique concepts mainstream and rob the boutiques of much of their novelty? When will

Paris goes to Vegas. With a little help from Schonbek.

The new Paris Las Vegas casino and mega-resort carries out its theme with a passion that is positively French.

Guests gaze upon the Arc de Triomphe, the facade of the Louvre and the Eiffel Tower (scaled down, *un peu!*). The cuisine, the shopping, the decor—*Oh! là! là!* But what makes the crowd stop and stare is the dazzling display of Schonbek crystal chandeliers in rooms that the 17th century monarch Louis XIV might have mistaken for his own.

67 Maria Theresa style crystal chandeliers and 198 crystal wall sconces illuminate scenes that recall the Château de Versailles and the Hall of Mirrors.

Authenticity was everything to the project owners. Schonbek won the bid over European competitors based on quality of crystal and integrity of design. For example, we went to our own antique catalogs to revive the Maria Theresa styling in all its glory.

Schonbek traces its history back to 1870 in Bohemia.

If you have a lighting assignment that's too unusual to be handled out of a catalog, contact us.

FREE VIDEO "BEYOND LIGHTING": CALL 1.800.836.1892

SCHONBEK®

Schonbek Worldwide Lighting Inc., 61 Industrial Blvd., Plattsburgh NY 12901-1908.   Showroom in Dallas TX, by appointment.
Tel: 800.836.1892 or 518.563.7500   Fax: 518.563.4228   www.schonbek.com   email: sales@schonbek.com

twentysomethings and their admirers tire of being hip? While nobody knows the answers, the fact remains that there will always be some guests who feel more comfortable in larger, full-service branches of established global hotel chains, while others will consciously choose smaller, limited-service and frequently idiosyncratic hotels under local management and ownership. No matter where they register, they are likely to be surrounded by good architecture and interior design.

Roger Hill of the Gettys Group observes that the conservative, risk-averse hotel industry retains a deep-seated fear of trendsetting despite the extensive restructuring that has made it lean, focused and profitable. The last decade saw a wave of consolidation as U.S. hotel companies bought one another, extracted economies out of redundancy and inefficiency, and found new savings in transforming the way it developed and operated properties. But there is more work to be done, Hill points out, as hotels build on their new benefits and advantages to create powerful brands that customers know, trust and prefer. Europe is perhaps 10 years behind the U.S. in this regard, but the opportunities are the same.

So the age of vanilla, chocolate and strawberry restaurants and hotels has come to a close. Let us welcome the age of passion-fruit, white chocolate macadamian—and other flavors we have yet to realize we want. Whatever comes next, our hospitality accommodations are going to be delicious.

Roger Yee, an architecture graduate of Yale School of Architecture, has received honors for his work in the field from such organizations as the American Institute of Architects, The American Society of Interior Designers and the Association of Business Publishers. He has been editor-in-chief of three design magazines, Corporate Design & Realty, Unique Homes *and* Contract Design. *In the latter capacity, he created InterPlan, the New York interior design exposition held each autumn since 1994.*

His other activities in the field have included being marketing advisor to Cushman & Wakefield, a national real estate firm, serving as draftsman and designer to architecture firms, most notably Philip Johnson and John Burgee, and lecturing on design at institutions of higher education including Dartmouth College and Columbia University. He is currently editor-in-chief of b3, *a magazine about e-business, and consultant on editorial, public relations and marketing issues to numerous organizations in the design community.*

AT LAST, BUSINESS AND PLEASURE LIVING IN HARMONY.

MANUFACTURERS OF FABRICS MADE OF FR POLYESTER FROM KOSA MUST BE AUTHORIZED TO USE THE AVORA™ TRADEMARK

DESIGNED BY BRAD ELIAS, ELIAS DESIGN GROUP INC. NEW YORK, NY

AVORA™ FR | KoSa

FOR MORE INFORMATION CALL: 704.586.7525 · WWW.AVORA.COM

Crystal Seduction

Trend

featuring Swarovski
Spectra Crystal

Sensuous chandeliers of exquisite design as only Bernard Pecaso can create them.

- **Exclusive Designs**
- **Custom Creations**
- **Spectacular Re-Creations of Historic Chandeliers**

All Pecaso chandeliers feature a higher density of crystals (more crystals per inch), superior quality crystals (Straas, Swarovski and our exclusive Hermitage crystals), and our renown value.

Call for free product literature or a personal appointment.

Bernard
Pecaso
The Art of Lighting

Bernard Pecaso Lighting, Inc.
395 Wythe Avenue, Brooklyn, NY 11211
Ph: 718•599•4579; Fax: 718•963•2868

SHOWROOMS: •DALLAS •CHICAGO •NEW YORK •TUPELO •HIGH POINT •BROOKLYN

CATALOGUES AVAILABLE - TO THE TRADE; SHOWROOM LOCATIONS NATIONWIDE

Edward Ferrell 569-84

Lewis
MITTMAN
LEWIS MITTMAN INC.
D&D BUILDING,
979 THIRD AVE,
NEW YORK, NY 10022
(212) 888-5580
FAX: (212) 371-5061

Edward
FERRELL
EDWARD FERRELL LTD.
685 SOUTHWEST STREET
HIGH POINT, NC 27260
(336) 841-3028
FAX: (336) 841-5280

Lewis Mittman 2060

Lewis Mittman 9860

Edward Ferrell 631

Edward Ferrell 198

HOSPITALITYDESIGN

THE
PREMIER
MAGAZINE
FOR THE
HOSPITALITY
DESIGN
INDUSTRY

■ HD2001 EXPO & CONFERENCE, LAS VEGAS

March 29-31, 2001

May 2-4 2002

 For Expo information call 312.583.5609

■ www.hdmag.com

Online Buyers Guide

Editorial Calendar

■ For Subscriptions, call 847.647.7987

or fax 847.647.9566

EDITORIAL OFFICES

770 BROADWAY

NEW YORK, NEW YORK 10003

T. 646.654.7450   F. 646.654.7626

imagine,

create

THE VITON CHANDELIER

INTERNATIONAL
IRONWORKS, INC.®

THE LIGHTING MANUFACTURER   TEL 323.262.9936   WWW.INTERIRONWORKS.COM

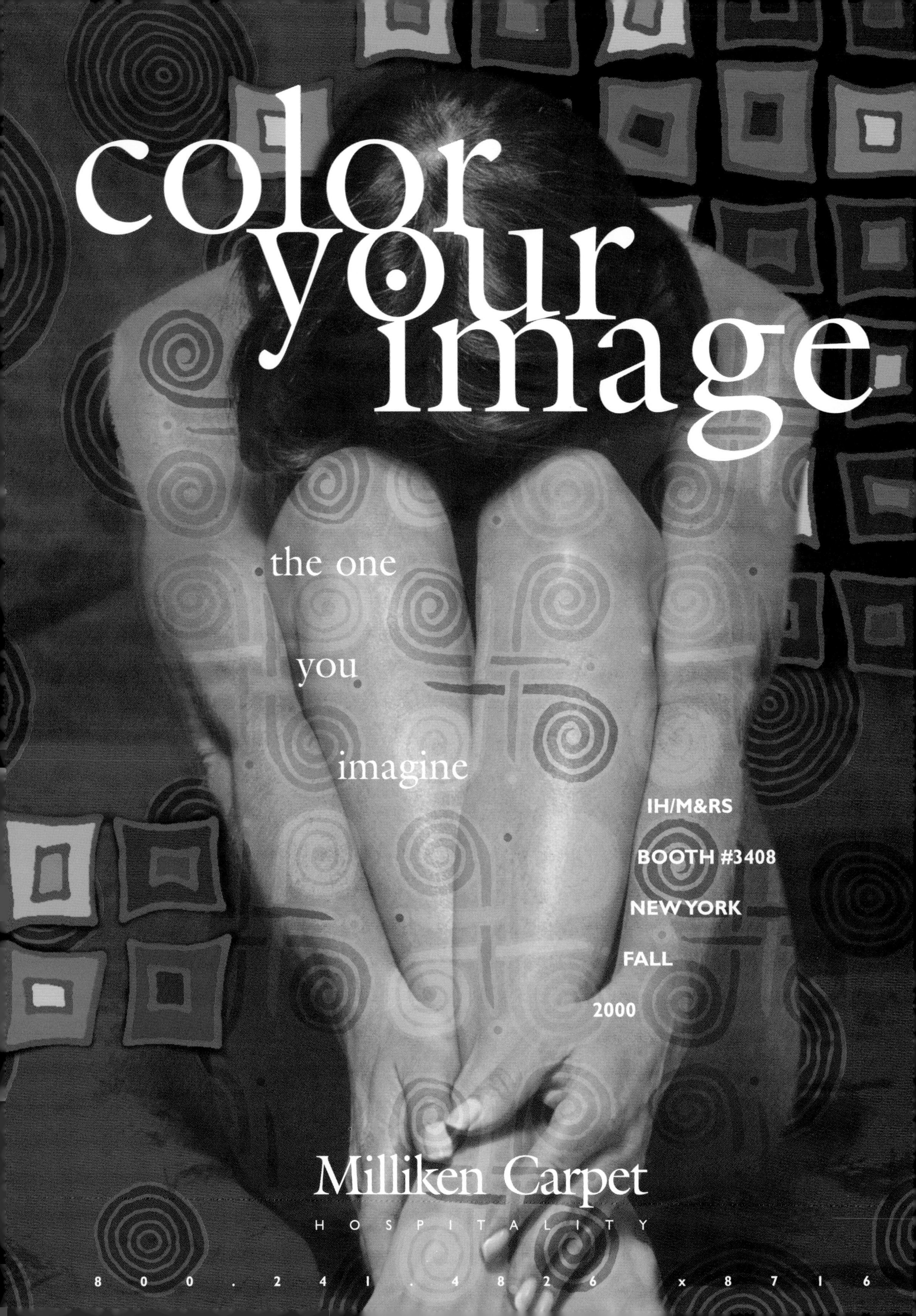

color
your
image
the one
you
imagine
IH/M&RS
BOOTH #3408
NEW YORK
FALL
2000
Milliken Carpet
HOSPITALITY
800.241.4826 x8716

Index of Advertisers

Index by Projects